LOGAN
ALBRIGHT

OUR SERVANTS, OUR MASTERS

HOW CONTROL MASQUERADES AS ASSISTANCE

AMERICAN INSTITUTE FOR ECONOMIC RESEARCH

Our Servants, Our Masters

How Control Masquerades as Assistance

By Logan Albright

ISBN: 978-1-63-069188-2

Design: Vanessa Mendozzi

to Marty, and Victoria's

Logan Albright

LOGAN
ALBRIGHT

OUR SERVANTS, OUR MASTERS

HOW CONTROL MASQUERADES AS ASSISTANCE

AIER | AMERICAN INSTITUTE *for* ECONOMIC RESEARCH

"In a mature society, 'civil servant' is semantically equal to 'civil master.'"

~ Robert A. Heinlein

Contents

INTRODUCTION

The concept of hierarchy is so natural that it worms its way into virtually every aspect of life. Continually frustrating the dreams of a certain sort of Utopian thinker for a wholly egalitarian society, there emerge everywhere leaders and followers, servants and masters. Most of us have to submit to a boss at work; some of us have employees who have to submit to us. Parents rule the household while children, in theory anyway, have to do as they are told. Among groups of nominally equal friends, one person will usually emerge as the one who sets the agenda, or whose lead the others tend to follow. This is all very natural and not, in itself, a bad thing.

When hierarchies go awry is when we fail to recognize them for what they are. An employee who thinks he is equal to his boss is likely to land himself in trouble. A father who does not exercise at least some authority over his children is likely to throw his household into chaos. A servant who thinks he is master is in for a rude awakening indeed.

Usually, this is not a problem, as leaders are generally happy to make their role in society evident to all. However, there is a certain class of hierarchy that exists in modern America, in which the servant-master relationship has been turned on its head, and like something out of Alice in Wonderland, has confused the great majority of the public about what is really going on. The root of the problem can be found in the term "public servant."

Without wishing to get too ahead of myself, let me just say that this term has had the insidious effect of tricking millions of people into believing they are in charge of situations, over which they actually have little or no control. There is a reason for this. People like to feel in control. It is a feeling that banishes fear and uncertainty. It is a feeling that most of us are all too happy to embrace when given half a chance, even when it doesn't reflect reality. It is also a feeling that breeds complacency. It is when we feel in control, when we let our guard down, that we are actually most vulnerable.

It is the aim of this book to show that much of the control we feel in our everyday lives is actually an illusion, and more than that, a deliberate deception perpetrated on us in order to preserve a certain status quo.

While some readers may find this a depressing conclusion, I'm happy to report that it's not all bad news. Individuals, as we will see, actually function very well through voluntary cooperation and close-knit communities. We don't actually need public servants to serve us, as they claim to do, or to lord over us, as they actually do. We can get along just fine without them. Therefore, the problems elucidated in this book are *solvable and unnecessary*. We just need to wake up and face the reality of the world we have built around us, and embrace a willingness to change things for the better.

It is my hope that the information contained herein will spur readers to take back some of the power they have gradually and unwittingly ceded to others, so that they may ultimately lead richer, more fulfilling lives. It's ambitious, I know, but why bother writing a book if you don't have something big to say?

Eureka Moments

There is a famous story about the Greek mathematician Archimedes. He had been presented with the problem of how to determine whether an object apparently made of solid gold were actually only *gold plated*, without actually cutting into or destroying the object itself. Archimedes was a brilliant man, but here he was stumped. Frustrated at his inability to solve the problem, he took a bath to clear his head. When he saw the way water was displaced by his body as he bathed, the answer suddenly struck him. Objects placed in water displaces an amount equal to their mass. Since a solid gold object will have a higher mass than an imitation, it is possible to determine gold's purity by measuring the amount of water it displaces. "Eureka," Archimedes cried, meaning "I've found it." He hadn't expected a bath to inspire one of his most brilliant discoveries, but it proves that you never know when inspiration is going to strike.

This is a book about Eureka Moments, those times when an idea suddenly hits you with so much force that your entire worldview is rocked by it. I have had many such moments in my own life, some great and some small, but each one broadening my viewpoint and causing me to see the world in a way I never dreamt of beforehand. Each such moment transformed me into a different person than I was before, and in each case the change is permanent. Once a Eureka Moment strikes, there's no going back.

I can still remember my first big Eureka Moment. I was ten years old, rifling through my parents' record collection to see if I could find anything interesting. Now, keep in mind that I was born in the early eighties, and at that time my musical experience had been largely limited to MTV-style pop and new wave, along with a smattering of oldies. I had never heard anything vaguely experimental or unorthodox. The standard pop song structure — verse. verse, chorus, verse, chorus — was all I had ever known.

As I browsed, one of the records caught my attention. The cover art depicted a burly barbarian on a motorcycle, bursting out of an open grave into an evil red landscape, surrounded by gothic tombstones and a large, grinning bat. The artist's name was Meat Loaf and the record was called "Bat Out of Hell." I would like to say I was intrigued by all this, but that would be an understatement. I was fascinated. Hey, I was a ten-year-old boy, can you blame me?

With reverence, I pulled the record out of its sleeve and placed it on my parents' turntable. After a crackle, the first guitar notes emerged from the speakers, and I was spellbound. The music was intense and complex, but the thing that really blew my ten-year-old mind was how long it went on uninterrupted by vocals. Nearly three minutes into the eight-minute song, the singer had still not opened his mouth. It had never occurred to me that such a thing was possible. I was familiar with instrumental music from classical composers and the like, but the idea of a song, a rock song no less, that expended a third of its length without singing was new to me.

I became obsessed with that record. I still listen to it every so often today, and it ultimately led me to a lifelong love of music, particularly the strange and experimental. Once my rigid ideas of what was acceptable in rock were shattered, I fell in love with novelty and creativity.

Since that day 25 years ago, I have had many other Eureka Moments, usually brought on by some book I happened upon that exposed me to a new way of thinking. Some of those books can be found in the bibliography of this one, should you be interested in seeking them out and seeing whether they reach you the way they reached me. You no doubt have had many such moments from your own life, unique to your own vision of how the world works.

Over time, what I came to notice was that my Eureka Moments all shared a common theme. They were not unrelated sparks of insight, although at first it seemed that way. They were pieces of a larger puzzle, only removed from one another because I was missing the central piece that condensed many little revelations into one big one. That revelation was the consistent, predictable relationship between a stated desire to help others and an actual desire to control them.

Beware of servants; all too often, they end up really being masters.

PART ONE
Education

There are few members of modern American society more revered than teachers. While some may revile the police officer who protects the innocent and sneer at the doctor who saves lives, few indeed are those who dare say a word against these venerable public servants. We lament their chronically low salaries, their difficult working conditions, and their lack of political power. Never mind that the teachers' unions are among the most powerful in the country, and that getting fired for being a bad or even abusive teacher is next to impossible. Facts, ironically, are irrelevant to our understanding of the education system.

We're supposed to hire teachers in order to enjoy the benefits of their wisdom, which they pass on to us in the form of instruction. A teacher who fails to teach, or whose wisdom has been exhausted, gets the sack. This is the theory, but as everyone knows, the reality is quite different. When teachers are not feared by students, they are instead subverted by attempts to cheat, get out of assignments, and otherwise undermine the authority of the instructor. How strange! No one tries to subvert the authority of a janitor or a maid. You don't hire someone to wash your car, and then hide the car from them so they can't find it. But people treat teachers like this all the time. The cliché holds that actions speak louder than words, and the way people behave towards teachers clearly demonstrates that we don't actually see teachers as the public servants they profess to be, whatever our language may tell us. Instead, we view them as authority figures, capable of controlling our actions and inflicting punishments on us if we disobey. We lash out at them, at least the ones brave enough to lash out, to demonstrate our independence and unwillingness to be controlled. It's the same attitude some people take towards policemen, tax collectors, and anyone else trying to tell us what to do and when to do it. Simply put, we rebel against authority. We don't rebel against subservience.

Before you get the wrong idea, this is not meant to be an indictment of teachers. I myself have enjoyed the benefit of several wonderful teachers. Indeed, I owe my current career and life path to some of them. I have also worked as a teacher during parts of my own career, so I have at least some minor understanding of what these people go through. But I wish to draw a distinction between actual teachers, and those who merely bear the title. The public school system does not actually encourage teaching. It encourages crowd control, conformity, and the production of a class of citizens capable of passing standardized tests and little else.

To teach a willing student is indeed a noble and praiseworthy thing. It is rewarding to watch knowledge grow and ability blossom. I daresay all too few professional teachers get to experience this very often, given the constraints of the public education system. Wonder is rarely a byproduct of compulsion. To force knowledge down the throats of an unwilling, captive audience is not really teaching at all. It is indoctrination, propaganda, and brainwashing. The public servants whom we trust to educate children more often take the form of petty tyrants, demanding obedience and the repetition of officially-sanctioned truths, not to be questioned or contradicted under threat of poor grades or, worse, expulsion.

It shows how far down the rabbit hole we've gone when the most severe punishment for students who find school hateful and miserable is that they might not have to go anymore. Excommunication from the church of schooling is so socially fearful that many would rather continue to suffer within the system than try to make their own way outside of it. It's Stockholm Syndrome for the young, and it's a classic indicator of how the servant-master relationship has been turned on its head.

Not that I blame the teachers themselves. They have little choice, being employees of a system that they have little hope of influencing, much less changing. The training they receive, combined with the situations into which they are unfortunately placed, limit their chances of becoming genuine purveyors of education to the young minds in their charge. Enormous class sizes, administrative structure, and the demands of standardized testing give them few opportunities to legitimately inspire and motivate students. And the fact that the vast majority of these students are forced to attend classes against their will certainly doesn't make things easier.

All this is combined with a general attitude of collectivism in regards to our children. There is a sense, bolstered by public officials cramming it down our throats every chance they get, that children are not individual human beings with the same rights and privileges as the rest of us, nor are they the wards and responsibilities of their parents. Rather, they belong to the state, the only entity that can be trusted with such a valuable natural resource. Hillary Clinton, always hostile to the nascent homeschooling movement during her time as First Lady, first of Arkansas and then of the United States, declared that *It Takes a Village* from her perch atop the bestseller list. In other words, it is not for you to raise your children; it is for us to raise them.

Years later, this sentiment was echoed by MSNBC host Melissa Harris-Perry, who made headlines by declaring that "we have to break through our kind of private idea that kids belong to their parents, or kids belong to their families, and recognize that kids belong to whole communities."[1] Many parents were understandably shocked at the idea that they have no more claim over their children than anyone else in the community, but this is not a new point of view. In fact, it is one that has been creeping towards the forefront of American consciousness for over a century.

In his *Principles of Ethics*, published in 1887, the British philosopher, biologist, psychologist, and political theorist Herbert Spencer wrote:

"We have fallen on evil times, in which it has come to be an accepted doctrine that part of the responsibilities [of child care] are to be discharged not by parents but by the public — a part which is gradually becoming a larger part and threatens to become the whole. Agitators and legislators have united in spreading a theory which, logically followed out, ends in the monstrous conclusion that it is for parents to beget children and for society to take care of them."

The doctrine is even more accepted now than it was in Spencer's day. In the face of such collectivist thinking, it's no wonder that we have given schools and the people who work in them such all-encompassing governance over our children.

But what is the alternative? What choice do we have but to trust our kids to this ineffective, overpopulated system where individuality is sacrificed to conformity? It may seem that we have no other options, but that's merely because, for the last 200 years, we haven't seen any counterexamples to the status quo of compulsory, universal schooling. Or at least most of us haven't, but that's only because we haven't been looking closely enough.

---

1 Holly McKay, "Critics Slam MSNBC Host's Claim that Kids Belong to Community, Not Parents," *Fox News*, April 9, 2013.

Growing Without Schooling

Growing up, I didn't go to school.

I like telling people this, in no small part for the pleasure of seeing their expressions of shock, horror, and confusion. But it's completely true. I went to college and I went to graduate school, but before that, I never spent a single day inside a school. "Oh," people sigh, breathing a sigh of relief. "You mean you were *home-schooled.*" Well, yes, but not in the way they are thinking of. When most people conjure up the mental image of homeschooling, they picture children sitting at a kitchen table, being actively instructed by their parents, filling out exercise books and taking tests, earning grades, and dividing their day into specific subject areas, just as they would in a public school classroom. Not so for me.

My parents practiced a form of education known as "Unschooling." It's an educational philosophy pioneered by former-school teacher John Holt. Holt observed that cramming a bunch of children of the same age into a room and demanding they learn things based on a rigid, arbitrary schedule didn't work all that well. He saw the spark of curiosity and wonder in infants and toddlers gradually get snuffed out as the education system turned learning from a joy into a chore. Unschooling dispenses with curricula and testing, and instead allows children to explore the world at their own pace, learning only what interests them or what they need to know to achieve a specific goal, such as attending college or getting a job.

Sound crazy? I know from experience that to most people it will. We've been trained to think that public, compulsory education is the only way to keep our children from growing up into gibbering illiterates. Along the way, we've been taught to revere teachers as practicing the most noble of professions, and to unquestioningly accept that more government spending on education is always a good thing. After all, investing in education is investing in the future, right? The answer depends on what you mean by "investing" and what sort of dividends you expect the future to yield.

How Children Learn

When a child is born, its parents get a handful of years with it while it learns how to walk and how to speak, and various other necessities for human interaction. Once that business is taken care of, the child must go to school, where it will learn all the little things necessary to live a good, productive, and fruitful life, until it is grown up enough to fend for itself out in the big, bad world. In short, the parents are expected to surrender a large portion of their child's life over to the institution of schooling within a few years after creating it.

This expectation is near-universal in modern America, but my parents didn't do that. When it came time to surrender me into the hands of the authorities, they said, "No." And thus, the course of my entire life was changed from what it might have been.

Why, we must ask, would my parents take a position so contrary to what all their peers, neighbors, and relatives had done? Why would they reject society's call, at the risk of depriving their firstborn child of all the benefits a good education could provide? What could inspire such madness?

In short, they wanted to spare me their own experiences in the education system. They wanted to spare me a childhood full of bullying, humiliation, and being made to feel inferior just because I might be different. Difference, they realized, is not some deformity to be punished, but rather something to be nourished and celebrated.

If what we tell our children is true, that they are all special, unique, individuals, then why do we insist on treating them in exactly the same way as everyone else? Individual children require individualized education. That much should be obvious.

Let's back up a bit. A few paragraphs ago, I mentioned children learning how to walk and how to speak. If you have children yourself, take a moment to visualize how that process took place. If you don't, think back on your own childhood or the childhood of someone else you know. There were no classes in walking. There was no exam demanding that babies be able to crawl by a certain age or be held back a grade. No one sits infants down and lectures at them about how to curl the lips and position the tongue to form the sounds necessary for speech. No one drills words into children, "cat, dog, mommy, daddy," to make sure they learn them. Kids figure all this stuff out on their own, simply by watching the people around them and imitating what they see. Of course, interaction is required. Parents need to encourage their children when they get things right or make a good effort, so that they know they are on the right track. Babies, it has been shown, can't actually learn to speak from watching television. They have to have the feedback of human communication. But that feedback needn't, and doesn't, take the form of formal instruction with a curriculum and rigorous testing.

The obvious question is; how do children do this? You may argue that it's instinct, and not analogous to more abstract learning like mathematics or history. There is some truth to that; language and walking on two legs are more or less innate features of our species. But just because something is instinctual doesn't mean it doesn't have to be learned. In the rare cases when children have been isolated from other people at a young age, we find that language doesn't develop at all. And even in the best of circumstances, language acquisition is an arduous process that takes years of constant practice and trial and error. Instinct accounts for some of it, but there is also a concerted effort to learn something that is difficult, but useful, and more importantly, tremendously interesting. If children can learn to crawl, walk, and speak without being actively taught, it's not unreasonable to expect that they can learn other things as well.

Let's try an experiment. Go up to a five-year-old boy and ask him to tell you everything he knows about dinosaurs. Go ahead, I'll wait. Finished? It's just as likely you got bored and cut him off long before he ran out of information. Where did he get it from? There are no dinosaur classes, at least not at the pre-kindergarten level. No one sat the kid down and demanded he memorize the names of every species from A to Z. No one warned him he had better remember them all, because a test is coming next week. He learned it the only way anyone really learns anything well, because he was interested in it, because it was fun, because he *wanted* to learn.

Everyone who has spent time around small children has observed this phenomenon. Kids barely old enough to talk will expound for hours on whatever their current obsession happens to be. Apart from the astonishingly vast amount of information retained, one cannot help but be impressed by the pure passion with which these juvenile lectures are delivered. Children this young have not yet been taught that learning is tedious or laborious; they think learning is the best thing in the world, and it is.

If we accept that the very young are capable of learning a huge amount on their own initiative, why do we suddenly forget this when it comes time to enroll them in school? Why must force be suddenly and unyieldingly applied to a mind that was already soaking in its surroundings like a sponge?

The reality is, children's thirst for knowledge doesn't just spontaneously dry up when they reach the age of six (or five, or four, or three, or whenever the increasingly omnipresent schooling bureaucracy demands they start showing up to classes). I know it doesn't dry up because I've seen it in children of all ages, with the only thing they have in common being the fact that they haven't had the love of learning beaten out of them by relentless assignments, grades, and tests. Contrary to popular opinion, children are not naturally lazy, only wanting to pass their time with television and video games. Schooling makes them that way, by systematically teaching them that reading, mathematics, and books of all kinds, are the stuff of unpleasant duty rather than grounds for endless exploration and play. Their natural inclination is to learn, and keep on learning.

Education Versus Schooling

Lest the reader misunderstand, this is not a paean to ignorance. I happen to think a good education is one of the most important and rewarding things in life. Education is what allows us to become more productive, to improve our standard of living, and ultimately to fulfill our dreams. The importance of education is widely understood, so there's no need to dwell on it here, but what does need clarification is the logical leap between wanting children to be educated and requiring them to attend institutions known as schools.

Schooling and education are very different things, although the words are too often used interchangeably. Education is the acquisition of knowledge, whether practical, theoretical, or historical. Schooling is the process of being taught things by an instructor, in most cases unrelated to the wishes or interests of the child.

Schooling can result in education, but it is neither a necessary nor a sufficient condition for it. Just as often as not, schooling deadens natural curiosity, replacing it with anxiety and self-doubt. The necessity of constantly comparing students against one another has some unpleasant side effects. Those who lag behind the average are made to feel stupid and inferior. Those who surge ahead are, in the best case, bored, and in the worst case, mocked and bullied for their success.

If you watch the news, you'll hear again and again that there is an epidemic of violence in our schools. Mass shootings are on the rise, and no one can figure out why. You'll hear explanations ranging from too-easy access to firearms, the over-prescription of Ritalin and similar drugs for children, a lack of strong families, violent movies and video games, and many others. Everyone has a theory on why children turn violent, but no one seems to ask what to me is an obvious question: why does this violence so often manifest itself in schools? Why not at home, in shopping malls, in public parks, at a friend's house, in restaurants, or on public transportation? Children are present in all these places, and yet they don't routinely shoot them up in the same way that they take out their aggression in school.

My opinion is that it's no accident that so many mass shootings occur in schools, as opposed to other popular gathering spots for the young. Schools are where children are forced to confront their deepest insecurities, their most loathed adversaries, and a crushing authoritarian rule, day after day, for the better part of their first two decades of life. Children are, almost by definition, comparatively powerless, a frustrating condition that is only compounded as more of their natural freedoms are stripped away. If an adult finds himself in an unpleasant environment, around people who are mean to him, who ridicule him, who make him lose his temper, he is free to leave. He can find a different job, move to another city, even get a divorce. Children in school lack these options. They have to return to the same building again and again, without respite, regardless of their feelings about the matter, or face legal penalties. Under these circumstances, it would be amazing if some *didn't* completely snap under the strain.

Another downside of schooling is that it doesn't seem to work all that well. In his book, *The Case Against Education*, economist Bryan Caplan collects a staggering number of statistics demonstrating that the vast majority of what students are taught in school is quickly forgotten. I'm sure we've all known people who have spent many years studying a foreign language in school, but who remain unable to utter more than the most basic of conversational clichés. Retention rates for everything that doesn't see continued practice on a daily basis is close to zero. Why might this be? It's certainly not true that the human brain is incapable of retaining large amounts of information. The five-year-old dinosaur enthusiast disproves that easily. So why do schools fail at teaching things students will actually remember? The answer is simple: the students don't care. We remember what we are interested in. We forget what bores us. The rub is that, while the boring can seldom be made interesting, the interesting can easily be made boring by forcing people to study it when they are in the wrong frame of mind, the wrong age, or in the wrong mood. If you want your five-year-old to forget everything he knows about dinosaurs, test him on that knowledge. Then keep testing him until he can't stand it anymore.

Soon enough, his expertise will evaporate into indifference, and, eventually, resentment.

At this point, the reader will be likely to object. "You can't just let kids study what they are interested in! They need to know certain things, whether they want to or not!" There may be some truth in this, but in fact the number of things kids "need" to know is much smaller than people assume. When is the last time you used the cosine function or needed to know the date of the Norman invasion? When's the last time you were called upon to speak French or calculate the surface area of a sphere? Unless you work in a very specialized field, odds are you will never need any of these skills, so why does society demand that you develop them, often at painstaking length? They certainly are not needed to acquire a good job and provide for oneself, nor are they strictly necessary to be a "well-rounded" individual, whatever that means. In fact, if we were really concerned with rounding students out, we would demand they all study different things, instead of the same ones. Diversity, we're told after all, is a strength,

While children are miserably disciplined into learning some things they will never use, other things, extremely useful things, get neglected entirely. Rare indeed are the schools that teach kids how to invest wisely, fill out a job application, write a résumé, fix an electrical problem, pay taxes, or change a tire. We're expected to master these skills on our own, without help, even though failure to do so can mean financial ruin, jail time, or in certain extreme scenarios, death or serious injury.

It is thus tacitly conceded that children are, in fact, capable of learning things without officially being taught them. Yet this is a truth that must never be uttered out loud, for if it became common knowledge, what then would happen to the motivation for continuing to fund and enroll in public education?

Pedagogy

Since society has decided that extensive schooling is really, really important, it's no surprise that an awful lot of time is spent arguing about how that schooling should be conducted. How many days out of the year should children attend school? How many hours out of the day? What kinds of technology can improve outcomes? How much testing should be done? These are all questions that get endlessly asked, but never really answered, largely because the decision-making process is based on politics rather than facts.

It follows that if being well-schooled is essential to being a good citizen, then the countries that school their children best will have the best citizens. If there's one thing America hates, it's losing to other countries, and so we obsess over international rankings to find out how our kids stack up against those around the world.

Usually, we don't do too well on these indices. According to the 2015 PISA rankings, conducted by the OECD, the United States ranks 25th in the world for science, 23rd for reading, and 37th for mathematics.2 Not exactly what you want if your country claims to be the greatest in the world. But rather than question the methodology of the studies and wonder how you can really compare as abstract and nebulous a concept as "education" across individuals, much less across countries, the powers that be freak out and insist that we must be doing something wrong, and that the solution

2 "PISA 2015: Results in Focus," *OECD.org*, 2018.

must therefore be to do more of it (this is the kind of logic that Washington, DC runs on).

It has been proposed that we do away with summer vacations for students and hold school year-round, that we get rid of recess periods to increase the amount of classroom time, that we introduce iPads and other high-tech gadgets into our schools, that we test more, that we put children in school at ever earlier ages, and that, above all, we spend more money on schools. How much more money? Doesn't matter. Just more. Always more.

It seems strange that doubling down on a failing system is the first instinct of policy makers rather than scrapping the status quo and trying something new, but changing course, thinking creatively, and embracing risky new ventures are the provinces of entrepreneurs, not of politicians and bureaucrats. Despite certain political slogans I could name, "change" is not something of which most elected officials are capable.

Fortunately, for those of us who wish to challenge the status quo, the data is on our side. If doing the same thing doesn't work, doing more of the same thing won't either. This is what simple logic predicts and this is, in fact, what we see when we look at the evidence. Fifty years ago, children in public school were doing about as well as they are now. The government, in its infinite wisdom, deemed this to be "not good enough" and sought to correct the problem. Until that time, education policy was set solely by states and localities. The federal government was considered to have no jurisdiction over the nation's schools.

There was good reason for this. The United States Constitution, which specifically lists the areas in which the federal government is legally permitted to act, makes no mention of schooling or education at all. Whether this is because the founders specifically wanted to deny this right to the government, or whether it never even occurred to them that such a threat was possible (more on this in the next section) is unknown, but one thing is for sure: our founding legal document doesn't permit federal involvement in the schooling of children.

Never one to let laws get in the way of a good power grab, President Jimmy Carter established the Department of Education in 1979, with the goal of overseeing the states and making sure their education policies all measured up to a national standard. The fact that this was blatantly unconstitutional has not stopped the Department from ballooning over the last forty years.

With that ballooning has come more funding, more staff, and more intervention from the top down. The rate of spending per student in the United States has skyrocketed.[3] The Department of Education employs thousands of workers, all ostensibly devoting their lives to improving schools in this country, and has a budget of $68 billion a year. George W. Bush's No Child Left Behind program was supposed to standardize educational programs and make sure poor or disadvantaged children didn't slip through the cracks. But in 2017, the Department of Education issued a report concluding that $7 billion in new spending had had no measurable impact on student achievement.[4]

Barack Obama's Race to the Top program doubled down on the idea, awarding grants to states that implemented certain reforms. This led to the much-reviled Common Core standards, which forced

---

3 Malcolm Getz, John J. Siegfried, "Costs per Student over Time," *National Bureau of Economic Research*, January, 1991.

4 Brooke Singman, "Education Department Report Finds Billions Spent under Obama Had 'No Impact' on Achievement," *Fox News*, January 25, 2017.

schools and teachers to follow particular practices whether or not they worked. Deviation from the norm was met with funding cuts, and few indeed were the states that dared to fight back against these federal incentives.

So backwards were the standards that they demanded children solve math problems that were literally unsolvable, not due to difficulty or advanced theoretical concepts, but because of how poorly the questions were written and conceived. Common Core pedagogy includes demands that children abandon calculation in favor of estimation, and students who get the answer correct are marked off for excessive precision. Because of the uniform standards, a textbook monopoly has arisen, in which there is only one option if schools wish to conform with federal guidelines. Some of these textbooks have been accused of teaching revisionist history, taking a particularly one-sided, anti-American view on the events of the 18th century. And while there's nothing wrong with teaching about historical atrocities and tragedies when they occurred, schooling can easily turn into propaganda when the other side of the story — the good and noble contributions America has made to the world — are ignored entirely. This problem underscores the importance of competition, in which a variety of ideas and approaches are offered, with the best and most popular options prevailing over ones that people hate. The textbook monopoly resulting from federal meddling in education policy presents only one version of events, and given that history is not so much the study of what happened as an *interpretation* of what happened, it's rather crucial that alternative interpretations are available.

Parents who object to what their children are taught are left with few options. Since all schools must be the same, according to federal fiat, switching to another classroom is unlikely to produce a better result. Private and religious schools remain out of financial reach for many families, and homeschooling requires a certain time investment on the part of the parents that can be unrealistic. Nevertheless, a surge in the numbers of homeschoolers since the practice became legal in the 1980s (before that, mothers were actually being locked up for attempting to educate their own children) indicates a widespread dissatisfaction with the system as it exists today. As of a few years ago, homeschooled students in North Carolina outnumbered those attending private schools,[5] and survey data indicates that the primary reason parents choose to homeschool is a concern over the environments of public and private schools.[6]

It's no wonder people are dissatisfied. In spite of all the increased spending, employees, and federal control — or maybe because of it — educational outcomes have not improved. If anything, we seem to be slipping behind other nations, at least according to the standardized tests that measure such things. Putting kids in school at younger ages doesn't work either. We're constantly told that it's important for our children to get a head start, to start learning early so they get a jump on their peers, and are ready to enter the real world, head down and running. But the evidence fails to back this up. The federal early-childhood education program known, fittingly, as Head Start was supposed to get students learning earlier in order to give them a boost throughout their lives. For a few years, it seems to work. But these gains disappear as the children get older.

5 Bob Adelmann, "Homeschoolers Outnumber Private-School Students in North Carolina," *New American*, September 9, 2014.

6 Sean Cavanagh, "Data Snapshot: Who Are the Nation's Homeschoolers?", *EdWeek Market Brief*, November 20, 2017.

A study commissioned by the same people who run Head Start, and who therefore have a vested interest in proving that it works, concluded that all measurable gains from the program disappeared by the time the kids reached third grade.[7] On any sane planet, this conclusion would be grounds for terminating the program, yet it keeps right on rolling, with more funding than ever to bolster its nonexistent results.

What are we to make of this? Why is it that spending more money, devoting more resources, and injecting all the latest technology into classrooms doesn't make students smarter? Maybe it's because we have a particularly flawed understanding of pedagogy to begin with, and maybe public schools have never really been about educating at all. Maybe there's another purpose behind them altogether.

School of Rock

Call to mind some of history's greatest thinkers. You'll probably come up with names like Pythagoras, Socrates, Aristotle, Newton, Galileo, Da Vinci and so forth. How did these men get so bright, how did they learn so much, how did they unlock secrets that eluded the rest of the world? Genius may never be fully understood, but one thing we do know about these men is that they did not spend their childhoods sitting in classrooms, taking exams, and being numerically compared to every other child their age. They had no computers. They had no calculators. For the most part, they either learned by doing, or else by someone telling them things while

---

7 "Third Grade Follow-Up to the Head Start Impact Study," *Office of Planning, Research, and Evaluation*, October, 2012.

standing on a rock on some lonely, windswept mountainside.

It is true that these men were outliers, genetically blessed with intelligence, but nevertheless we can extrapolate that, given the right pupil, all you really need to nurture the mind is a good teacher, a few books, and a rock to sit on. The obvious follow-up question is, what makes the right pupil?

The easy answer is to dismissively classify the world's philosophers, scientists, and theologians as fundamentally different. Pedagogy doesn't matter for these brilliant people, you might claim. They would have flourished no matter what situation they were put into. We need to concern ourselves with the average, or indeed the below average, student. Those are the people who need society's help, not the gifted ones.

If you accept the purely nature-based theory that some children are gifted and others are dull, then I suppose this attitude makes sense, but what if it's more complicated than that? What if a stifling and stultifying childhood snuffs out many potentially gifted individuals before we have the chance to see them flourish? What if pedagogy does matter, just not in the way we think it does?

You probably played with one of those so-called Chinese finger traps when you were a kid. You stuck the index fingers of both hands into a tube of woven fibers, and when you tried to pull them out again, you found yourself stuck. The harder you pull, the tighter the tube becomes, and the only way to escape is to relax the pressure entirely. This appears to be a good analog to the way human brains work. The harder you try to force knowledge into them, the more they resist; the more freedom you give them to learn on their own, the faster they become educated.

A couple of real-world examples will be helpful at this stage.

In Finland, a country that routinely performs well on international education rankings, schools have banned the use of iPads and other electronic learning aids.[8] Far from inhibiting learning or holding back students, the absence of an electronic crutch has reportedly allowed students to focus more on the teachers and the lectures, without being distracted by shiny playthings. If you've attended college in the last 20 years, you're no doubt familiar with the PowerPoint Professor, that sort of teacher who, instead of actually engaging his students in thoughtful conversation and debate, spends an hour flipping through a slide show of various disconnected bullet points, graphs, charts, and equations. Some students like this sort of teacher, because rather than attend class, they can simply download the slide show, memorize it at their leisure, and ace the test. Other students, the ones who actually expect to get an education along with their degree, hate them, because bullet points are not a substitute for real learning.

Keeping on the theme of technology, I came across an interesting project authored by the XPRIZE Foundation. For those who don't know, the XPRIZE Foundation is a non-profit organization that attempts to incentivize major breakthroughs with large cash prizes. They post a series of challenges related to things like space exploration, medical research, and energy production, and offer huge sums of money to anyone who manages to achieve them. This is intended to be an alternative to government-funded grants, outlining specific goals rather than just endlessly funding research that may not go anywhere. I'm a fan of their work.

One project in which the XPRIZE Foundation has become

8 Caitlin Emma, "Finland's Low-Tech Take on Education," *Politico*, May 27, 2014.

involved in has to do with education in Africa. The Foundation recognized that, given the number of underserved students in African countries, it is simply not possible to build enough schools or train enough teachers to continue the traditional model of education with any degree of efficacy. So instead, they are pursuing a different approach, one which relies on the assumption that children are able to teach themselves more quickly and effectively than is commonly assumed.

Currently in the testing stage, XPRIZE has challenged researchers to develop open-source tablet software to be deployed in African countries, designed to allow children to teach themselves the basics of reading, writing, and arithmetic over the course of 18 months.

Matt Keller, senior director of the Global Learning XPRIZE described the project this way:

"These tablets will be given directly to the children with limited to zero instruction. If kids can't figure this out on their own, these solutions won't scale. We are not relying on adults. Based on work I did in Ethiopia with Nicholas Negroponte from MIT and One Laptop per Child, Maryanne Wolf from Tufts, and Cynthia Breazeal from MIT, I am somewhat certain that children will figure out how to use the tablets very quickly."[9]

The XRPIZE challenge relies on the knowledge unschoolers have had for decades, but which has continued to elude education policy experts: children are natural learners. All they need is the opportunity.

But wait a minute, doesn't this contradict my earlier point?

---

9 Toby Shapshak, "Using Tablets in Rural Africa, XPRIZE Hopes to Inspire Education," *Forbes*, April 29, 2016.

I argued that the Finns improved schools by removing tablet computers, but that Africans can benefit from them. How can both of these be true? The answer is that the Finns were reacting against the use of technology as a substitute for good teaching, whereas the African experiment involves learning about technology independently. I'm not saying that technology has no place in learning. In fact, the internet is the greatest tool for autodidacts since the printing press. I'm merely pointing out that technology alone can't replace a wise old bearded man lecturing from a rock.

A Dragon with No Gold

Let's go back to those tests I was talking about earlier, the ones which compare children across international borders so we can know whether we're smarter than the Belgians or the Swiss. Americans worry a lot about these tests, especially since we tend to get clobbered in them, but we rarely take the time to ask what is actually being tested, and whether the results are useful or meaningful in any way.

The first thing you should know about tests is that they really only measure one thing: how good kids are at taking tests. Just as the most successful politicians are not the ones who are best at governing, but the ones who are the best at getting elected, the most successful students are not the ones who learn the most, but the ones who best figure out which boxes to tick on the provided form.

There's no better example of this than the practice of "teaching to the test" which has arisen in schools as a result of standardized testing and federal incentives. Here's how it works: schools are given extra funding based on how well their students do on exams. School administrators then inform teachers that their students must do well on exams, or else. The teachers then suspend any efforts they may have made to actually educate children, and instead start teaching them how to score well on exams. In extreme cases, teachers actually encourage their students to cheat, or cheat on their behalf, in order to raise scores and thereby increase funding, handing out test answers to the class before the exams in order to permit easy memorization, or actually changing wrong answers by hand on exam papers. This is what happened in a high profile case from Atlanta, in which 178 teachers and administrators were caught changing students' answers, a practice that had been going on for as long as a decade without detection.[10]

It doesn't matter that rote memorization is basically unrelated to actual education in the sense of learning how to think; all that matters is that the students look good on paper.

This begins to explain why the United States scores relatively low on international comparison tests, and yet has one of the highest rates of invention and entrepreneurship in the world. If tests actually measured intelligence or education, we would expect a strong correlation between test scores and personal achievement later in life. The pupils who did best on tests would reliably grow up to be our Einsteins and our Bill Gateses. But, as most everyone knows, this correlation doesn't exist, at least not nearly at the strength we would expect it to. Albert Einstein was famously a bit slow in school, bad at chess, and late even to childhood speech. Bill Gates, as well as being one of the world's richest men, is also America's most famous college dropout. A lack of a diploma was no obstacle

10 Steve Osunsami & Ben Forer, "Atlanta Cheating: 178 Teachers and Administrators Changed Answers to Increase Test Scores, " *ABC News*, July 6, 2011.

to his success, and who knows what would have happened if he had spent the last of his college years stuck behind a classroom desk rather than obsessively learning everything he could about the then-fringe technology of computing? Windows might never have happened at all.

China, along with other East Asian countries, tends to do very well on international comparisons of education. This has led to calls from American policymakers to imitate the so-called Chinese model here at home. We should all become "tiger moms", pushing our children harder, tending towards hyper-competitiveness, and letting go of outdated notions like free play and "just being a kid." Asians perform so well on standardized tests that colleges in the United States actually practice reverse affirmative action against them, denying qualified candidates spots on the student roll in favor of others from less successful racial groups. Imagine if we allowed discrimination of this kind against any other race. The outrage would be tremendous. Yet the Asians put up with it, and still manage to fill up our colleges and universities by being at the very top of their classes. Clearly, they must be doing something right, right?

Well, not necessarily. It depends on what your goals are. While it's true that Asians score well on tests and make good grades in class, once they leave the classroom and enter the real world, the picture gets a bit murkier. Asian countries rank poorly in entrepreneurship and in the rate of patents acquired by their citizens. And in some countries, like Japan, a large proportion of the adult population languishes in purposeless unemployment, video game addiction, social isolation, and even suicide. In his book, *Who's Afraid of the Big, Bad Dragon?*, educator Yong Zhao explains why we see this disconnect between success in school and success in the real world.

He writes, "Authoritarianism has driven America to admire, glorify, and emulate other authoritarian education systems because they seem to produce 'results,' defined as test scores. Instead of valuing what their own educational methods can produce, American leaders envy countries with top test scores in a narrow range of subjects — which is simply a sign of how successfully those countries have homogenized their students." He goes on to say that "China, the perfect incarnation of authoritarian education, has produced the world's best test scores at the cost of diverse, creative, and innovative talents" and describes America's eagerness to emulate the Chinese model as "suicidal."

The Chinese model of education stresses extreme discipline, effort, conformity, and collectivism. Success is not credited to the individual, but to the whole society, whereas an individual failure creates shame for the whole family. Children are not encouraged to follow their dreams and reach for the stars, but to buckle down and work, work, work to avoid bringing embarrassment to their parents.

Creativity is not emphasized, because creativity doesn't show up in the statistics.

You may have seen an Asian violinist or pianist with flawless technique, executing the most rapid and difficult passages with ease. This is not surprising, as classical music education is a priority among Chinese families, with children expected to practice multiple hours a day. But at the same time, you may have felt that something, the emotional core of the music, the passion, was missing. That's because passion cannot be arrived at through meticulous obedience to the sheet music. It has to come from a place of creativity within. The fact that there is no Asian equivalent to Mozart or Beethoven is no accident. Chinese musicians are simply trained to think in a different way from European and American ones.

What Zhao explains in his book is that this methodology emerged as a way for families to cope with his country's historically authoritarian governments. Children were driven like slaves to excel in school because that was their only chance of escaping grinding, perpetual poverty, not because the Chinese model of schooling produces better, smarter adults. What began as a survival strategy to cope with tyranny and poverty should not be mistaken for an enlightened pedagogy in a free society.

Why Is Education Important?

We are encouraged to look to the Chinese for inspiration, because their education model produces high test scores, but it is important to remember that test scores themselves are not the end goal, or at least they shouldn't be. No parent wishes their children high test scores at the exclusion of all else. Test scores are only important inasmuch as they accurately measure other variables that we actually care about, so the obvious next question is: what do we actually care about?

We want our children to grow up to be intelligent, successful, prosperous, and, perhaps most importantly, happy. But when we take our eye off the ball of these metrics, focusing instead on standardized tests, we are apt to miss the forest for the trees. There is no evidence that children raised in the Chinese model become wealthier, healthier, or happier than their peers. Most of the truly successful entrepreneurs, in terms of raw inventiveness and disruption — and as measured by financial success in the marketplace — have been Americans like Bill Gates, Steve Jobs, Jeff Bezos, Elon Musk, and Mark Zuckerberg. Most people's idea of a happy childhood does not include practicing the cello for four hours a day under the judgmental gaze of an authority figure, and it's hard to see any way in which adult Asians have, as a group, reaped the benefits of their strenuous childhoods.

But this leads us to a broader point about society's attitude towards education in general. Why is it prized so highly? Why has speaking out against more spending on school, or even the suggestion that the status quo needs to change, become a heresy? Bryan Caplan's research indicates that more schooling will generally translate into higher wages later in life, but he is quick to point out that this has less to do with the amount of knowledge acquired and more to do with signals sent to potential employers that applicants are capable of following orders, submitting to authority, and conforming to expectations.

If pure return on investment were the only thing at play, we would expect to see a radically different attitude towards education than what is expressed in every newspaper, every political speech, and every State of the Union Address. Trade and vocational schools are frequently more financially rewarding than liberal arts colleges; professions such as electrician, welder, machinist, and plumber are badly understaffed, so much so that many companies are actually willing to pay for schooling just in order to acquire qualified workers, workers who will then proceed to earn premium wages for jobs that badly need doing. Yet when the president, whoever he may be, goes on TV to urge young people to get an education, he doesn't mention these sorts of professions. Instead, he wants kids to double down on graduate school, or perhaps even go for a PhD. And although the STEM fields (Science, Technology, Engineering, and Math) are in vogue right now, he really doesn't care what you major in as long as you stay in school for as long as you possibly can.

One unfortunate consequence of the public pressure for universal education is that, as demand goes up, so do prices. Yes, it turns out that even august and noble institutions of higher learning are not entirely immune from the law of supply and demand. When too many kids are chasing too few spots in America's most prestigious institutions, prices are bound to rise. But the cash-strapped high school grad need not worry. Our benevolent government would never let tuition be an obstacle to the dream of college for all. Here comes Uncle Sam, ready to benevolently extend loans with very reasonable interest rates to youngsters still hoping to follow the president's sage advice.

The result has, predictably, been a tremendous surge in the amount of student debt in the country. Far from allowing young people to become liberated masters of their own destiny, the push for ever more education has led to an accumulation of debt that can only end in disaster. In total, American students now owe nearly $1.5 trillion for their educations, and over 44 million Americans hold at least some student debt.[11] That averages out to more than $30,000 per student. In many cases, students will never be able to pay off those loans for the rest of their lives, leaving them forever under the thumb of the government that told them college was important in the first place.

The student debt crisis will likely end in one of two ways. Either the bubble will burst, or the government will bail out students with apparently free money. In the first case, the realization that students will never be able to repay their obligations will inspire lenders to get

---

11 "A Look at the Shocking Student Loan Debt Statistics for 2018," *Student Loan Hero*, May 1, 2018.

out of the student loan business, driving interest rates up and drying up the supply of loanable funds. This will parallel the housing crisis of 2008, in which unsustainable debt caused a mass of foreclosures and abandonments, tanking the economy in the process. The same thing could easily happen with student loans.

The alternative is that government engineers a bailout, a student loan forgiveness plan in which borrowers are no longer obligated to pay back what others have lent them. On the surface, this may sound like the preferable option, until you recall that there's no such thing as free money — it has to come from somewhere. In this case, it will either come from taxpayers, who will be forced to finance the education of other people's children, or from the government simply printing more money, leading to inflation that makes all of our dollars worth less. In either case, it will only compound the problem, leading students to believe that there is such a thing as a free lunch after all, increasing the demand for higher education, raising prices even further, and necessitating the issuance of even more debt, which just leaves us right back where we started, except worse. It's a vicious spiral that cannot go on forever, and when something cannot go on forever, it typically doesn't. The results of an unsustainable situation screeching to a halt have, in my experience, never been pretty.

So why does government insist on inflating the price of liberal arts educations when the inevitable result must be a collapse? To give policymakers the benefit of the doubt, it could be simple ignorance, and a lack of thought for the future. The other possibility is that they want children to undergo university for the same reason they want children to undergo elementary school: to learn, not how to think, but how to think in a particular, state-sponsored way.

Crazy on Campus

If students are willing to go into so much debt to attend college, it would be reasonable to expect these to be pretty amazing places. The traditional image of higher learning involves free-thinking, bearded intellectuals pondering the great mysteries of life behind ivied walls. We picture rigorous discussion, debate, argument, leading to enlightenment and self-improvement. We tend not to think of tenured bullies demanding rigid adherence to a particular fringe ideology, hurt feelings, and a general prohibition on anything interesting that might accidentally get talked about.

By now it's impossible not to have heard the stories of the kind of lunacy that goes on on college campuses all over the country. Trigger warnings shield students from uncomfortable truths, free speech zones tacitly acknowledge that saying what you think elsewhere on campus is not okay, and Marxist professors punish students who disagree with their worldview using the twin rods of poor grades and public humiliation.

Think I'm exaggerating? In fact, 18 percent of social science professors in America self-identify as Marxists, more than three times the 5 percent who identify as conservatives.[12] Not just liberals or progressives: Marxists. You know, the ideology that resulted in the deaths of hundreds of millions of people in Russia and China due to massive famines, executions, and genocides.

These professors are teaching America's youth that America is an evil empire; that the terrorist attacks on September 11, 2001 were deserved; that the nuclear family is a form of white supremacy;

12 Jenna Lawrence, "AEI Panel: Marxists Outnumber Conservatives in Social Sciences", *Campus Reform*, June 13, 2016.

and that cultural appropriation is the same as physical theft.

A Facebook page called "Film Your Marxist Professors" regularly exposes so-called teachers taking outrageous, fringe positions such as calling for the violent overthrow of the U.S. government or falsely claiming that mass murderers like Josef Stalin didn't kill anyone.

This is what $1.5 trillion in debt buys our country. This is the system that every president insists needs more participation by young people. This, we are told, is the ticket to a successful life.

It should be clear that very little of the higher education system is actually about training students to be better critical thinkers. In an increasing number of cases, it's more about imposing a particular worldview onto a captive audience too inexperienced to know that what they are hearing is ridiculous nonsense. If this sounds conspiratorial, just wait. The history of public education has always been one that stresses conformity and indoctrination over actual learning. The evidence is there for anyone who cares to look. It's just that most of us don't bother. We imagine that education in America has always been this way, emerging fully formed on the new continent like Venus from Zeus. But it was not so, not even close.

The History of Compulsory Schooling

Believe it or not, schooling was not always compulsory, nor was it always the province of the government to educate society's children. In the broader context of human civilization, these remain relatively recent innovations, if they can really be called such. In his excellent little book, *Education: Free and Compulsory*, economist Murray Rothbard traces the history of compulsory education in Europe and America.

When colonists first settled on the American continent, not only were there no government schools, there were no schools at all. The British government was a three-month ship journey away, and so families had to figure out how to teach their children what they needed to learn. Mostly, this was done in the home, for the simple reason that most families could not spare the extra hands to help out around the farm, or whatever else the family business happened to be. Today, we shudder with horror at the thought of child labor, but the historical norm has always been for children to work as soon as they grew old enough to make themselves useful. This was not out of cruelty on the part of parents or greedy capitalists, but out of necessity. Survival, until very recently, has been an extremely difficult objective, and no hands, however small, could be spared in reaching for it. Children worked because if they didn't, the whole family risked starvation. Children learned what they needed to learn to survive, or else they didn't survive. It was a harsh world, but not a complicated one, at least.

As the Industrial Revolution made us wealthier and less apt to die, families gradually began to have more options. Those with the most money, who didn't have to send their kids to work in factories or coal mines, started to teach their kids more refined skills beyond the bare essentials needed for survival, skills like reading, writing, music, art, history, philosophy, language, mathematics, and everything else we expect kids to learn today. All well and good. Education, after all, broadens the mind and opens up a world of possibilities, as long as it doesn't come at the expense of growing enough food to stave off starvation through winter.

The early history of schooling outside the home involved little one-room schoolhouses where children could go to learn from members of the community who would volunteer their time to teach them. Everything was voluntary, and if a family didn't have the time or resources to spare, their children were free to help out around the home instead of being forced into a classroom against their family's wishes.

Contrary to what you might think, this time period was not one of uneducated squalor. Literacy rates in the early history of the United States were quite high, even when compared to today. It seems that children functioned well in this environment, or at least tolerably so. Then came the Germans.

Germany was an early forerunner of the concept of compulsory education. It all began with Martin Luther and his split from the Catholic Church. At that time, Catholics were content to hold religious ceremonies in Latin, taken from Bibles, also written in Latin, regardless of whether the general public could speak the language or not. Priests were relied upon to interpret the word of God and convey it to those who could not read it themselves. The people would then pray to the priests, who would then relay the message to God and offer absolution — or not— on His behalf.

Luther was none too happy with this system, believing that people should be able to communicate directly with God, and consequently should also be able to hear His word in the common vernacular, in this case German. Since Lutherans were expected to be able to read their own, German-language Bibles, it should come as no surprise that literacy was considered an important virtue for the spiritually devout. God's word was the key to salvation, reading was the key to God's word, and so to permit illiteracy was to tacitly accept damnation for an unacceptably high number of people. It was therefore the Lutherans who began to stress the importance of compulsory schooling for the greater glory of God and His subjects.

In the 16th century, Germany began to adopt compulsory schooling laws at the urging of Luther, who considered that his interpretation of the Bible, as opposed to the Catholic interpretation, should be taught to all children. It's tempting to argue that Luther just wanted people to be able to think and decide for themselves, but far more likely that he planned to use education as a form of reinforcing his own views on young people, just as it is used today. Luther expressed his attitude towards compulsory education thus, and it is telling that he analogizes it to conscription, another practice by which the state uses individuals against their will for its own ends:

"If the government can compel such citizens as are fit for military service to bear spear and rifle, to mount ramparts, and perform other martial duties in time of war, how much more has it a right to compel the people to send their children to school, because in this case we are warring with the devil, whose object it is secretly to exhaust our cities and principalities of their strong men."[13]

Following Luther's example, John Calvin, another religious reformer, began establishing schools with compulsory attendance to spread his own ideas about how a holy life should be led. It was Calvin's influence that would carry over into the United States, as Puritan colonists settled in early New England.

Compulsory schooling may have been designed to achieve holiness, but what it actually accomplished in practice was to reduce children's options and force them to conform to a standard set by the schoolmaster, whoever that might be.

---

13 Quoted in Murrary Rothbard, Education: *Free and Compulsory*, The Ludwig von Mises Institute, 1999.

The Prussian empire, famous for its militarism, embraced the idea of mandatory schooling following Luther, adopting a paternalistic view in which citizens were to be trained for the good of the nation. Rather than view schooling as a tool for promoting holiness, they viewed it as a good way to train an army, to teach children to follow orders, submit to authority, and grow up with a common understanding of what their king expected from them.

It's no coincidence that when the idea of compulsory schooling began to infiltrate the United States, or the colonies that preceded them, it began with the states with the largest Puritan influence. The Germanic desire for order and obedience, coupled with the Protestant ethic handed down from Luther and Calvin, ran deep in certain parts of the fledgling country. In the 17th century, Massachusetts was the first state to pass a mandatory schooling law, followed closely by its New England neighbors. It's notable that church attendance was also mandatory in Massachusetts at the time, showing how closely linked were the ideas of obedience to the church and to the state before the Bill of Rights demanded their separation.

The southern states, peopled as they were by more independently minded Scottish and Irish immigrants, took longer to acquiesce than the more strictly authoritarian New England states. By 1850, only Massachusetts and Connecticut had mandatory schooling laws. It wasn't until the 20th century that compulsory schooling became a nationwide phenomenon. If one takes the trouble to read through the various arguments made for establishing compulsory schooling, it is striking how much focus is put on obedience, uniformity, and religious indoctrination. Relatively little space is devoted to what we now think of as the values of public education, namely:

enlightenment, independence, and the development of practical life skills.

I remember the first time I learned about truant officers growing up. I was stunned at the idea that there were people out there whose job was to round up children, as if they were wild animals, and force them into government buildings against their will. As an early unschooler, I had to constantly be on my guard not to let myself be seen during school hours outside playing, reading, climbing trees, or doing any of the other things normal children like to do. Instead, I stayed indoors, still doing those same things, but confident that I would not be seized by a hostile stranger and dragged away from my family.

The transition from schools as instruments of religious indoctrination to instruments of government indoctrination followed a similar path in the United States as it did in Europe. Puritan ethics gave way, as the state grew and the church receded in importance, to instructions on how children could best be used to serve the interests of the nation's government. Ask not what your country can do for you, but what you can do for your country, frequently heralded as a profound statement of patriotism, could well have been the rallying cry of public schools in the early 20th century with only one small change: replacing the word "country" with the word "government."

Where Do Your Loyalties Lie?

Have you ever thought about the Pledge of Allegiance? Where did it come from and why do we say it? Who wrote it, and why do we insist that children perform this ritual recitation at school of all places? Why not at home or at church? In fact, the Pledge of Allegiance was written by Francis Bellamy, a socialist and nationalist who campaigned for a government takeover of the economy.[14] The Pledge appeared in the late 19th century at the dawn of the "progressive" era in American history, an era that few people talk about today, because the truth is so ugly that it's easier to cover it up. More on that later.

If you actually take the time to listen to the pledge, there are clues to its origin. *I pledge allegiance to the flag of the United States of America.*

Why to the flag? Why not just to the United States themselves? A direct endorsement of one's country would seem to make more sense than the more convoluted symbol worship of promises to be loyal to a piece of cloth with a pattern printed on it. But then, flags have traditionally been used as military symbols, as a banner under which the troops could be rallied to action. The nature of this action is, of course, unspecified. All that is expected is that you obey, without question.

And to the Republic for which it stands.

Here again, instead of stating love for or loyalty to one's country, the pledge requires that you support the Republic, the government. And since a government is itself no more or less than the men who run it, what we are actually requiring our children to say is that they will serve and obey whoever happens to be in power, a rather self-serving initiative on the part of the people who fund the schools, don't you think? I wonder how many people, reflecting on the current President of the United States, would feel comfortable with that promise if they really thought it through.

---

14 Gene Healy, "What's Conservative about the Pledge of Allegiance?", *Cato Institute*, November 4, 2003.

The rest of the Pledge's text is more or less harmless (some people quibble over the "under God" part, but that was added later and not part of the original text), but the first two lines are creepy enough for me that I refuse to say them. I can't help but think of little North Korean children being made to stand up and give thanks to their glorious leader who, according to his own propaganda, can do no wrong. It doesn't help that the original version of the pledge was said with the arm raised in a gesture most of us would now recognize as a Nazi salute. Any government that has to demand loyalty in this way from little children certainly doesn't deserve it.

The militaristic flavor to schooling doesn't end there. Odds are, you've taken so many multiple choice tests in your life that you've never even considered a time when they didn't exist, but there was such a time, and it wasn't all that long ago. It turns out that standardized, multiple choice tests were developed by the psychiatrist Robert Yerkes and sold to the U.S. military during World War I as a way of quickly sorting through thousands of potential soldiers and determining who was acceptable.[15] These tests were not designed to help soldiers flourish, but rather to give the army an easy way of arranging hierarchies within the ranks. Test takers were not unique flowers whose individuality had to be nurtured, but cogs in a machine that needed to be rapidly sorted into various pigeonholes. The tests every child takes today were never intended to help them learn. They exist to help the powers that be tell the wheat from the chaff, where wheatiness is defined as the ability to follow orders and regurgitate material on command. The fact that

15 Ainissa Ramirez, "The Dark History of the Multiple-Choice Test," *Edutopia*, May 20, 2013.

the military found no value in the results from Dr. Yerkes' tests didn't stop them from becoming mainstays in the school system of the 1920s, where they remain virtually unchanged a century later.

Schools as Laboratories, Children as Rats

If you haven't been convinced by now that the education system is not designed to serve children, but rather to mold them into what the teachers, administrators, and bureaucrats want them to be, then consider this final data point. A few years ago, the Department of Education issued a report outlining the goals of current education policy. Most of the report is predictable and mundane; things like increasing standards, integrating technology, and recalibrating the way testing is done. One section, however, stands out as particularly frightening.

People generally hate bureaucrats because they are cagey and indirect. They never say what they mean and they speak in that political doublespeak that manages to use lots of big words without really saying anything. Every once in a while, however, you find an overly enthusiastic employee who accidentally lets his true intentions slip. You have to watch for them, but they do exist. In this case, the author of the report, so excited about the potential of new technologies in the classroom, forgot to conceal what he was really planning.

In a rare moment of candor, the report argues that facial recognition software could be installed in classrooms to monitor students at all times. The software would scan faces to detect levels of interest, eye movements, facial expressions, and screen for potential mental illnesses like attention deficit disorder or autism.[16] That's right, the goal of the education bureaucracy is to have a computer decide that if your son looks out the window too many times in class, he must have ADHD, or that if your daughter doesn't smile or make eye contact enough, she might be autistic. Tell me that's not a terrifying thought.

Worse yet, this data would be housed on a government server, potentially forever. Forget any notion of privacy you may have ever had. The word loses most of its meaning when the government can access every citizen's eye movement patterns from age five on up. The lust for such data is evident in comments like the one made by then-Secretary of Education Arne Duncan, who wished aloud for an Orwellian system of tracking students throughout their entire lives. In a speech before a research conference, he said, "Hopefully, some day, we can track children from preschool to high school and from high school to college and college to career."[17]

Believe it or not, schools are actively being used to spy on, track, and ultimately control our children, and if they aren't now, they soon will be. Such is the desire of the people who continually tell us that any cuts in education spending, any reduction in federal involvement will result in disaster and calamity the likes of which we've never seen before.

The whole process is reminiscent of a new system being implemented in China today: the Social Credit Score.[18] Chinese citizens

---

16 "Promoting Grit, Tenacity, and Perseverance," *U.S. Department of Education*, February, 2013.

17 Arne Duncan, "Robust Data Gives Us the Roadmap to Reform," *U.S. Department of Education*, June 8, 2009.

18 Rachel Botsman, "Big Data Meets Big Brother as China Moves to Rate Its Citizens," *Wired*, October 21, 2017.

are currently being assigned scores based on their actions, whether they vote, how they do in school, their level of community participation, etc. Citizens with high scores are rewarded; those with low scores are denied services such as air travel. The government gets to decide who is and who isn't worthy of basic goods and services in the marketplace. It may seem like a stretch to imagine such a system in the United States, but one thing is for sure. You can't have Citizenship Scores without an extensive surveillance apparatus that tracks citizens over the course of their whole lives. The public school system is increasingly resembling just that sort of apparatus.

Our Teachers, Our Masters

At its worst, the school system serves as a tool to train good little conformists and indoctrinate children into believing a particular version of the truth. But just as often, parents rely on schools for a more benign, but equally depressing purpose. In a society where two-income couples are the norm rather than the exception, parents need something to do with their kids during work hours. In the minds of many, school has ceased even pretending to be an institute for improving children's minds, but merely a place to keep them occupied while other caregivers are busy. Teachers are no longer trained to teach, but to babysit, to keep classrooms full of children busy for the sake of keeping them busy.

Even in the best case scenario, when the affected children don't resent the control and don't suffer any psychological consequences from bullying, humiliation, or lack of academic success, there is still a significant opportunity cost in merely occupying entire generations of people. Think of the waste of giving millions of kids eight hours of busy work a day, five days a week, for a minimum of 12 years. Think of what else could be accomplished in that time, not just in terms of actual learning, but in terms of contributions to society, helping with the family business, volunteer work, acquiring meaningful skills, and a host of other things we haven't thought of yet.

Instead, we treat our kids like unwanted prisoners, to be kept at bay rather than nurtured. We call the prison guards teachers and we praise them for their contributions to society. We demand that the wardens command higher salaries. We argue that sentences should be extended until they approach life, that yard time should be limited, and that parole should be taken off the table. A friend of mine even wryly observed that the school he went to was actually designed by a prison architect. And why not? The goals are the same: population management, and ultimately behavior control. There's just one crucial difference between schools and prisons, and that is that the inmates of the former have committed no crime apart from merely existing.

PART TWO
Economics

Economics may seem a strange subject for a book about help and control; most people think of economics as the study of money, stocks, bonds, business structure and international trade, and this can scarcely have any relevance to the subject at hand. In fact, economics is much more important than people realize, and a thorough understanding of its principles will be necessary for the chapters that follow.

Economics is not the study of money, but rather, the study of scarce resources and choices people make between mutually exclusive alternatives. The term "scarce" in economics does not mean "rare", but "finite." In other words, if the consumption of a resource by one person lessens the amount available for others, this resource is called scarce. It will be easy to see that almost everything, with the possible exception of ideas and knowledge, falls under this category.

It therefore falls to economists, as well as other types of scientists, to determine how well we as a society are doing, and to come up with solutions to the problems that prevent us from achieving that happiness which each of us is encouraged to pursue.

In academic circles, there is actually some debate over this. Some theorists hold that economics is merely the study of how people do behave, not how they ought to behave, and that consequently it can make no value judgments, no distinction between good and bad, desirable and undesirable. This purely descriptive form of the science is called "positive economics"

Others counter that there are certain things we all have in common, such as the preference of life over death, prosperity over privation, and health over sickness. They therefore argue that the task of economists is to make life better for the individuals within a society by coming up with more efficient allocations of resources and attempting to maximize those variables we all consider to be good. This is called "normative economics."

In practice, almost all economics is normative. People don't hire economists because they want to better understand the human condition, but because they want to figure out how to achieve a particular outcome. A government may employ economists to figure out how to most efficiently raise revenue, or a business might employ one to determine how to maximize profits through changes in price and packaging size. In this sense, economists are servants, who try to make life better by solving problems and optimizing results. But the question is, whom are they really serving?

It's very rare for an individual to employ an economist to help manage the household budget or explain the opportunity cost of choosing one job over another. On the other hand, businesses and governments employ legions of them. In most cases, their goal is not to make life better for you and me, but rather to separate us from our money and modify our behaviors, often in ways so subtle that we don't even notice until it is pointed out to us.

Since science is held to be objective and economics is held to be a science (both statements are debatable), the economist is a useful tool for imposing an agenda without looking like you're imposing an agenda. The use of spreadsheets and equations provides a stamp of legitimacy for what ultimately boils down to opinion and preference. And since economists tend to be anonymous drones working in the background rather than flashy celebrities, politicians, or other public figures, it is easy to ignore their conclusions when they get in the way of what the bosses really want to accomplish.

Today, it is more common than ever for economists to occupy themselves, not with describing how markets work or predicting the outcomes of certain policies, but rather in telling people how they ought to live, as well as devising punishments and other disincentives for those who don't fall in line. But I'm getting ahead of myself. The first step in controlling behavior is differentiating between the desirable and the undesirable, and the first step in doing that is to devise some way of quantifying "the good." It sounds simple enough, but it has proven a remarkably thorny issue for economists for centuries.

How Well Off Are We?

Because resources are scarce, there will always be people who have less than they would like. Below a certain level, we call this poverty. When too much labor chases too little work, we call this unemployment. It has fallen to the modern economist to concern himself with these problems and devise, if he can, solutions. When economists try to make people better off, rather than confining themselves to the pure realm of education and understanding, they are forced to find some way to measure their relative success or failure. A unit of measurement is required for human well-being. Different schools of thought have dealt with this in different ways over the years, though none satisfactorily.

Money may seem an obvious yardstick of success, until you realize that there are many valuable things in life, such as family, religion, and leisure, that cannot be measured in dollars. In order to address this difficulty, the utilitarians, following the lead of Jeremy Bentham and John Stuart Mill, dreamt up an imaginary unit called the "util" to describe value. The more utils you have, the better off you are. The only problem is that there is really no such thing as a util, making it rather useless as a measuring stick.

Some analysts, determining that wealth is really less important than happiness, have tried to measure happiness directly. You have probably seen studies claiming such and such country is the happiest in the world, and wouldn't it be great if we could be more like them? Of course, measuring happiness is as futile as attempting to observe the invented util. The only way you can find out how happy someone is is to ask him, and as anyone who has ever worked in the legal profession will know, eyewitness testimony is seldom reliable.

In short, we can't self-report our happiness to researchers, because we don't really know how happy we are. Happiness is relative to our experiences. Someone who was born into wealth and has never experienced want is likely to be less happy than the poor kid who made good, simply because he has no experience to contrast his own with. Not knowing how painful life can be, he has no reason to appreciate all that he has got. Similarly, someone living in an impoverished country may be happier than we would expect him to be, simply because he has no experience of what he is missing out on. His happiness is not the same as our happiness; they cannot be compared, certainly not numerically.

Using happiness as a policy variable creates perverse outcomes. The parents of small children will never be happier than when they discover that their precious offspring, while thought lost or injured, are actually safe and sound. This does not mean that we can improve human well-being by kidnapping children and then returning them a short time later.

Today, most economists rely on the term "welfare" and hope

not too many people ask questions. Welfare economics is focused on optimizing this nebulous quality of "welfare," to make the most number of people as well off as possible. There are really two problems with this, both of which are largely ignored by professional economists.

The first of these, as we have already seen, is that there is no objective way to compare welfare between individuals. The second is that economics is not a science that lends itself well to optimization, if it can even be called a science at all. Let us explore these two errors in more detail.

The Paradox of Value

Economic orthodoxy has a long history, with most people regarding Adam Smith as the father of the field. Smith's famous work, *The Wealth of Nations*, published in 1776, asked the question of why some countries are rich and others poor, and served as a fundamental touchstone to later economic theory. From Smith's "Classical Economics" developed most of what is taught in university classrooms across the country today. However, Smith was not the first economist, far from it, nor were his theories definitive in the way most people believe. There are many valuable insights in Adam Smith's work, particularly his conception of how individuals acting in their self-interests can inadvertently benefit one another, and how the "invisible hand" of the marketplace regulates prices and production. But Smith had one great failing, and that was his inability to solve the Paradox of Value.

The Paradox of Value had long puzzled economists. The question was simply this: why are things worth what they are worth? Why is water inexpensive, when it is necessary for the continuation of life, but diamonds are expensive, when they have so few practical uses? Shouldn't it be the other way around? For centuries, the solution to this problem proved elusive. Smith's solution was that the value of a commodity was determined by the amount of labor that goes into producing it. Diamonds were expensive because they were difficult to mine, whereas water is easy to collect. This is the Labor Theory of Value, and it is very wrong.

To see why, imagine two competitors selling, let's say, chairs. The first is an artisan, a craftsman, who carves his chairs painstakingly by hand. It takes him a week to make each one, but they are very good chairs. Meanwhile, his neighbor employs an electrical machine to plane and shape the wood for him. He can fashion in minutes what takes the artisan days. At the end of the production process, both men have produced chairs of identical quality, which they then take to market.

Now, the Labor Theory of Value says that the craftsman should be able to command a higher price than his mechanized competitor. He poured blood, sweat, and tears into his work, so his product should, objectively, be worth more. Much to his dismay, he finds that his products command no such premium. The customer doesn't care how much time was spent making the chair, he only cares how good the chair is. If the artisan were to price his products based on the amount of time he spent on them, he would find few, if any takers. The Labor Theory of Value fails to predict the price actually observed. Since theories are only as good as the predictions they make, we can dismiss this explanation for why prices are what they are and start looking for others. Unfortunately, some ideas tend to stick around long after they are disproven.

Some decades later, a young German named Karl Marx seized on the Labor Theory of Value, and used it as the basis for his conception of communism. If labor creates value, then laborers are therefore the most important part of any commercial enterprise. From this point of view, the superior monetary rewards reaped by entrepreneurs, CEOs and managers seemed like a great injustice, which is why Marx advocated for workers to take control of the means of production and obtain ownership of that which they helped to create.

This fundamental misunderstanding of the nature of value is only one of the errors of communism and only part of the explanation for why it has failed everywhere it has been tried, but this example proves the power of ideas and the dangers of letting flawed theories go unchallenged for too long.

Smith's Labor Theory of Value has proven remarkably difficult to unseat from the popular imagination, although other schools of economics have been trying for more than a century. In France, the laissez-faire school of economics got a little further away from labor as the creation of value, but not all the way. Claude Frederic Bastiat, a brilliant economist who elucidated the unintended consequences of government interference in markets, believed that the value of a good or service was determined by how much it would cost the buyer to acquire it himself. For example, it is relatively easy for an individual to collect water from rain barrels or streams, but it would be an immense undertaking to seek out and mine diamonds. This is similar, but logically distinct from the Labor Theory of Value, and does a slightly better job of explaining real world prices, but inconsistencies still remained.

It wasn't until 1871, when an Austrian economist named Carl Menger wrote his *Principles of Economics*, that a true solution to the paradox of value emerged. What Menger realized is that value is actually determined at the margin, meaning that only the last unit consumed is evaluated at any given time. It makes no sense to talk about the value of water or the value of diamonds in the abstract; instead we have to look at the value of one additional unit of each commodity. If you already have a lot of something, one additional unit will not be worth very much, whereas if you are badly deprived of a good, you will be willing to pay more for just a little of it. Thus, water actually is more valuable than diamonds to a badly dehydrated desert traveler, but the man with plenty to drink has little to gain from one additional glass of water, and much to gain from his first diamond. This insight pointed economists to the idea that value is not an intrinsic property of certain goods, but that value can change relative to the situation, particularly with respect to the attitudes of consumers.

It's All Subjective

Since value determined at the margin varies considerably based on individual circumstances, it follows that value is a fundamentally subjective phenomenon. This was the most important insight of the Austrian School of economics, so named because of Menger's nationality, as well as a handful of influential followers whom we will meet shortly. Goods are not objectively worth anything. Their qualities, such as beauty and the amount of labor that went into them, are irrelevant as far as value is concerned. All that matters is what people will agree to pay, and what people will agree to pay depends entirely on their own subjective preferences.

This insight has profound implications for our understanding of human nature. If there is no objective measuring stick for value, then no one is in any position to tell anyone else what he *should* want, or that his preferences are incorrect. There is no such thing as "correct" when it comes to preferences, just as there is no "correct" value of consumer goods. What any person wants is particular to his unique circumstances, and largely beyond criticism. If a man prefers apples to oranges, you cannot say that he is wrong, only that you have a different preference than he has.

Of course, this has not stopped so-called experts from telling us what we ought to want in our lives. All too often, we still hear the accusation that someone is behaving irrationally, and that his preferences must be corrected "for his own good." The experts get away with this by claiming that we do not really know what makes us happy, what we want, or what will be good for us in the long term. Shortsightedness, ignorance, and even mental illness (about which much more will be said in the next section) interfere with our ability to make the "correct" choice, even though economics acknowledges that there is no such thing as correct when it comes to individual valuations.

Here is what Ludwig von Mises, a student of Carl Menger and one of the Austrian School's most powerful thinkers, had to say about these charges of irrationality:

"The assertion that there is irrational action is always rooted in an evaluation of a scale of values different from our own. Whoever says that irrationality plays a role in human action is merely saying that his fellow men behave in a way that he does not consider correct."

The above quote comes from the boringly-titled, but surprisingly interesting *Epistemological Problems in Economics*, in which the author attempts to determine how we can establish what is true and what is false in a discipline such as economics. He elaborates on the idea in his exhaustive treatment on the economics of *Socialism*:

"If a man drinks wine and not water I cannot say he is acting irrationally. At most I can say that in his place I would not do so. But his pursuit of happiness is his own business, not mine."

This is the theory of subjective value in a nutshell, the only theory that explains why prices are the way they are, and at the same time points out the futility of trying to use economics to direct individual behavior in "optimal" ways. That is, of course, unless you subscribe to the idea that what is important is not the individual and his happiness, but the welfare of society as a whole. This leads us into the perilous wilderness of trying to identify and incentivize "socially optimal" behavior.

Get Yer Utils Out

The search for the socially optimal is an outgrowth of the school of philosophy known as utilitarianism. Developed by John Stuart Mill and Jeremy Bentham, utilitarianism was an attempt to answer the age old question "what constitutes the morally good?" Bentham and Mill argued that the action which results in the greatest good for the greatest number of people is the morally correct one. Sounds good, doesn't it? Unfortunately, this definition raises more questions than it answers. What constitutes "good?" To the hedonists, good is defined as "pleasure," but other schools of thought found this too shallow a view, ignoring experiences that may be unpleasant but nevertheless good for spiritual or other reasons.

Even if we can agree on what is good, how do we calculate it numerically? In order to compare two outcomes, utilitarianism requires an equation that allows us to distinguish a good result from a better one. For that, we need numbers. Obviously, there are no units of pleasure, happiness, or any other commonly accepted definition of "the good." The neoclassical economist Léon Walras solved this problem by simply inventing an imaginary measuring stick and assuming it would obey mathematical laws in the same way other measurements did. Instead of "good" he used the word "utility" to describe how much satisfaction people would feel in their lives, and he dubbed one unit of utility a "util."

A person with ten utils is more satisfied than a person with nine utils. A person with 20 utils is twice as satisfied as someone with ten, and so on. The problem with this system should be obvious — there are no such things as utils in real life — but this has not deterred welfare and utility economists from embracing the idea in their efforts to optimize social benefits across the population.

Proponents of the Austrian School were quick to point out the absurdity of the utility concept, but even if we grant that there is a way to compare satisfaction across individuals, utilitarianism has another, perhaps more serious problem. It contains no concept of individual rights. If we regard life as good, then it becomes permissible to kill one man to save five, or to commit the most terrible of atrocities as long as the ultimate outcome justifies them with a greater good. The concept of a greater good has remained attractive to a large number of economists and social planners of all stripes, and it will rear its ugly head many more times throughout this volume, but it's morally questionable at best, and runs directly contrary to the philosophical principles upon which the United States Constitution was drafted.

America's Founders were chiefly inspired by the writings of

philosopher John Locke, not Bentham and Mill, and Locke had a strong conception of individual rights. He held that certain transgressions against one's fellow man were always wrong, regardless of whether they led to better long-term outcomes or not. This is why the Bill of Rights offers specific protections of rights such as the freedom of speech, the right to a fair trial, and protection from cruel and unusual punishment. Whereas a utilitarian might argue that cruel treatment of prisoners or stopping certain people from speaking could, in certain circumstances, lead to good outcomes, the American tradition holds that the ends, however noble, do not justify the means which treat human beings as mere tools in a grand design.

The legal structure, the very foundation of the United States, is therefore incompatible with utilitarianism, with the idea that it's okay to manipulate outcomes to produce an ideal result. It's no good to discuss making millions of people better off if doing so requires the violation of a minority's rights, and as author and libertarian Ayn Rand rightly pointed out, the smallest minority in the world is the individual.

The way social planners and economists have typically dealt with this problem is in one of two ways. The first is to simply ignore it, trample on the Constitution, and pretend that rights are of no importance in the face of the betterment of society. The second is to confuse the issue by advancing claims for competing rights — the right to health care, housing, a good job, internet access, and of course the rights possessed by "society" as opposed to those given to individuals. Such a cobweb conception of rights is clearly untenable, which suits the planners fine, since they would rather not deal with rights in the first place. In either case, a collectivist understanding of what is good for society takes precedence over what is good for any one person in particular.

The Myth of Society

I make no secret of the fact that I consider myself an individualist, perhaps even a radical individualist. This is not because I don't value other people, communities, families, or organizations. I do value these things, often very highly. It is not because I have fantasies of being a lone mountain man, pitting myself against nature with no need to depend on anyone else. I have always been a city dweller, because I recognize the immense benefits of trade, cooperation, and living close to other people who can do things that I myself cannot.

The reason I am an individualist is simply that without individuals, there can be no families, no communities, no organizations. All of these things are merely collective nouns that describe groups of individuals. In conservative circles, you will sometimes hear it said that the basic building block of society is not the individual, but the family. It's a nice sentiment, and the importance of strong families is undeniable, but logically, it makes no sense at all.

The nuclear family consists of individual members: the father, mother, son, and daughter. Each of these individuals is capable of acting independent of, and at times contrary to, the wishes or well-being of the family as a whole (by which I mean the consensus of all other family members). The family cannot be the basic building block when it itself consists of smaller units capable of acting on their own initiatives.

Ayn Rand argued that the concept of society itself was something of a myth; not that society doesn't exist, but that it's not analogous to an actual organism. Society can't take action, only individuals can, and society can't have interests beyond the interests of the individuals who make it up. It's a term people use when they want to avoid clear thinking and confuse the issue when the facts are against them. If a particular course of action benefits some individuals at the expense of others, it's easier to claim that society itself is at risk rather than argue why one group should be favored over another.

Italian economist Vilfredo Pareto attempted to solve the problem of competing group interests by identifying situations in which one party can be made better off without making anyone else worse off, a so-called "Pareto improvement," but in real life, cases like this are infrequent enough to make the concept of limited use outside of the classroom.

The acknowledgment that only individuals act is called in economics "methodological individualism," and it's a key tenet of the Austrian School. It clears up misunderstandings that emerge from using weasel words and foggy language. When someone claims that "the government collects taxes" what they really mean is that certain individuals within the government are collecting taxes. When we hear that the United States is fighting Syria, it really means that some American soldiers are shooting some Syrian ones. The United States can't actually fight anyone, because the United States is an abstract concept, not a person. Applying methodological individualism to problems like these can simplify seemingly complex issues by recognizing that we are all just people, not representatives of imaginary superstructures that have no physical, real world existence.

Scientism and the Progressive Era

At the end of the 19th century and beginning of the 20th century, the world was changing rapidly. Great strides were being made in scientific advancement, fulfilling the promise of the Enlightenment and leading great nations out of the shadows of ignorance and superstition using a lamp called the scientific method. Surgeons were learning to wash their hands, as germ theory emerged. For the first time, patients had a better than even chance of getting better when under the care of a doctor. Pasteurization was making food safer. New forms of transport and communication were emerging, and a man named Charles Darwin had a new theory about where we all came from.

Darwin's theory of evolution was controversial, but at the same time hard to argue with. When a monk named Gregor Mendel proved that he could selectively breed pea pods to encourage certain traits and discourage others, the idea of natural selection took a tight hold on the scientific community.

Of course, world-changing theories have world-changing implications. If progress in nature comes from survival of the fittest, from the strong being allowed to reproduce while the weak were allowed to die off, why shouldn't that same process apply to human society? And if we understand how the process works, why couldn't we — the scientists — change the rate of progress by conscious intervention in the breeding process?

I want to be clear that I don't blame Darwin or Mendel for any of what followed from their research. They were good scientists doing their best to uncover truth. Nevertheless, it cannot be denied that the discovery of natural selection led to some very peculiar ideas among some of society's wealthiest and most influential men.

With science heavily in vogue as a means of improving society, the idea began to emerge that we could apply the scientific method, not just to problems of physics and engineering, but to social problems as well. If science could build a better mousetrap, why not also a better society, a better economy, or a better human race itself?

This was the origin of the eugenics movement that swept the United States in the early part of the 20th century, chillingly chronicled by Edwin Black in his book *War Against the Weak*. Drawing from Darwin's theory of natural selection, those in positions of power — not just government officials, but wealthy industrialists like Andrew Carnegie — figured they could use the same principles to better mankind through selective breeding. Gregor Mendel had made pea pods grow taller by breeding out the weakness in shorter specimens. There was no reason society couldn't do the same for people. By choosing who was allowed to reproduce, within a few generations society should be made up of people who were taller, stronger, smarter, and more beautiful than humans had ever been before. The only problem was how to implement it.

The eugenicists had two tools at their disposal, the carrot and the stick. Some argued that incentive programs should be put in place, rewarding superior physical specimens who agreed to breed with one another, and subsidizing the resulting babies. Others focused their attention on preventing the genetically unfit — the stupid, the poor, the criminals, the mentally ill — from reproducing at all. In the end, the advocates of this latter practice found their scheme easier and more practical to implement. Over the next few decades, more than thirty states passed eugenics laws either forbidding breeding of certain people, or authorizing the state to forcibly sterilize those who were deemed unfit.[19]

This was utilitarianism at its finest. There was no question of what gave the state and its doctors the right to prevent certain people from having children. It was for the greater good, a more perfect

19 Edwin Black, *War Against the Weak*, Dialog Press, 2012.

society just a few generations into the future. What did it matter if a few eggs were broken along the way, when the resulting omelette promised to be so delicious?

In the Appalachian Mountains, where many poor families of Scottish and Irish descent had settled, people were dragged from their homes and sterilized without their knowledge or consent. Those who asked questions were told lies about minor, routine medical procedures. In some cases, they did not learn the truth about what had been done to them until decades later, after trying unsuccessfully to have children.

Incorrectly believing that criminal behavior was genetically transmissible, residents in the nation's prisons and mental hospitals suffered the same fate. All told, tens of thousands of Americans were denied the opportunity to reproduce, often without any form of due process whatsoever.

History textbooks rarely cover this part of American history, and I won't be surprised if this information is new to many of my readers. This is probably due to the fact that, in the 1930s, German scientists drew inspiration from what the Americans were doing. It was only after being fully exposed to the horrors of ethnic cleansing — the logical end point of eugenics — in the Third Reich that Americans began to back away from their selective breeding policy. Today, we rightly regard the practice as abhorrent, but forget that our own country planted some of the seeds that led to the Nazi Holocaust, all under the rhetoric of using science and objectivity to promote the greater good for society.

It's important to stress that the eugenics movement was not some lunatic fringe or radical splinter group. It was the mainstream position of American politics, and particularly the so-called progressive movement. Woodrow Wilson was elected President of the United States holding firmly pro-eugenics views, and the practice had the backing of both the medical establishment and the country's most influential businessmen. The position was an easy one to justify, because it had the backing of science, and science was always supposed to be objective, noble, and the way forward towards a better future. Who could argue with science?

This unfailing faith in scientists to solve all of the world's problems with numbers and pure reason is what is known as Scientism, the practice of blindly following the data without using morality or ethics as a safeguard against abuse. Implicit in scientism is the view that, whatever the current state of the art may be, the average layperson is compelled to assent and follow along without complaint. After all, he is no expert. How can he challenge the wisdom of those who know better? The fact that scientific consensus has been wrong more often than it has been right is rarely brought up, as is the objection that even when science does get things right, it doesn't mean we should blindly follow its conclusions.

From a strictly logical perspective, the eugenicists had a point. Allowing genetically transmissible disabilities to persist through breeding will, over time, result in a weaker society on average than if those traits had been allowed to die out. Their data and methodology, so far as it went, was not wholly incorrect. Where they went wrong was in sacrificing the human component, any conception of rights, morality, empathy, and compassion, to raw reason, and expecting everyone to just go along with them. The fact that eugenics is morally abhorrent does not, by itself, disprove the purely technical premises behind it. And that is what makes Scientism so dangerous.

Science Deniers

Before going any further, I want to clarify something. You may be thinking at this point that I am one of those so-called "science deniers," that my viewpoint is anti-science and anti-intellectual. Nothing could be further from the truth. Science is a wonderful — indeed, the best — tool mankind has ever come up with to uncover truth and solve complex problems. Science is the reason you and I are not starving to death, dying of exposure, poor, sick, miserable, and ignorant. Without science, you wouldn't be reading this and I wouldn't be writing it. We'd both probably be dead. Science is wonderful. I love science.

What I don't love is the notion that we should surrender both our reason and our compassion to men in white coats simply because they have a university degree, that we should blindly follow the advice of experts whom we are told are our superiors, that we should ignore the lessons of history and assume infallibility on the part of our scientists, and that we should apply the scientific method to areas of life where it is inappropriate to do so.

Contrary to popular belief, not everything in life can be reduced to an equation. Science is great at explaining fluid dynamics or photosynthesis. Science is less great at explaining ethics, kindness, or history. In cases where really smart guys have tried to treat these subjects in an entirely scientific way, the results have mostly been disastrous. More on this in a minute, but for now, end of sidebar clarification.

The Counter-Revolution in Science

You may be wondering what all this talk about eugenics has to do with economics, the subject of this chapter. The answer is that the scientistic approach to governance is a major part of what has gone wrong with economics over the years, with both progressivism and the eugenics movement falling into the same trap over and over again.

When scientists believe they have the keys to the universe at their fingertips, they frequently come to think that they can use those keys to design a societal structure from the top down, one that is based on logic and planning, rather than the apparent randomness that comprises nature and "primitive" societies. This is understandable. We don't content ourselves with living in trees, as provided by nature. We design houses. We don't resign ourselves to walking everywhere. We design cars and planes. Everywhere we look, human design appears to be superior to the state of nature. It seems that way, but this is actually an example of selective blindness, an inability to see that which does not conform with what we expect to see.

The benefit of naturally occurring structures, particularly when they are very complex with lots of variables, is that we know they work. If they didn't work, they would have ceased to exist years ago, but the fact that we see them around today means that they have survived environmental pressures and are efficient enough at least to still be around. There is an irony here in that survival of the fittest, the concept that led the scientific community in the direction of deliberate design, actually favors an approach that could more accurately be described as trial and error.

Trying to interfere with complex systems that have survived on their own for millions of years can have disastrous consequences, because as smart as we humans are, we lack the foresight to predict what exactly will happen when you make a deliberate change. A good example of this is the climate. Earth's climate is a staggeringly complex thing. It consists of millions of variables, from oceanic currents, to solar radiation, to greenhouse gases, volcanoes, domestic cows, plant life, clouds, evaporation, and so on. Attempts by scientists to model the climate and make predictions about the future have generally been failures. We can predict local weather patterns a few days or weeks out, but that's about it. There's simply too much going on for us to perfectly understand all the interactions taking place. Sometimes, things happen that we don't understand at all. For example, in the 1990s, the biggest climate crisis facing the world was the hole in the ozone layer. If you were around then, you probably remember scientists, politicians, and other talking heads fretting endlessly about what could be done. It was eventually agreed that hydroflourocarbons (found in some air conditioning units) were to blame, and the Montreal Protocol effectively eliminated these chemicals from consumer products.

Scientists predicted that, without hydroflourocarbons, the ozone layer would heal itself and return to normal, and for a while, that seemed to be the case. The most recent research, however, reveals that ozone levels in the lower part of the atmosphere have become increasingly depleted, while the upper level is seeing higher concentrations. This flies in the face of all previous climate models, and has left scientists baffled as to what is really going on. While the people who study ozone still insist the Montreal Protocol is working, they can't account for the changes in distribution and the overall continued decline in average ozone density over the last 20 years.[20] We just don't understand the atmosphere well enough to make accurate predictions about it.

---

20 Ethan Siegel, "Sorry, Earth, the Ozone Layer Isn't Healing Itself After All," *Forbes*, February 6, 2018.

On other occasions, smart people deliberately interfere with an eye towards making things better, and instead make things dramatically worse. This happens because they fail to foresee all the possible interactions in a system, and apply too shallow an understanding to their plans. A particularly stupid example comes from Chairman Mao's China. The communist dictator, seeking to supplant God Himself and remake China as he saw fit, undertook dramatic changes to the country's natural landscape. He ordered his people to redirect rivers from their natural flow. Observing that birds eat grain, he instructed Chinese children to deliberately kill off as many birds as possible, to preserve more food for the people. Mao must have been pretty pleased with himself when he came up with these plans.

Unfortunately for him, and even less fortunately for everyone else in the country, these modifications did not work as planned. Rivers that were redirected from rocky beds into more porous ground simply sank into the soil and disappeared. Without the birds to control the insect population, locusts devoured the crops, leading to the most devastating mass famine in history. Mao's arrogance in thinking he could redesign nature to suit his ends caused the deaths of tens of millions of people. And people wonder why we are skeptical of top-down solutions to complex problems.

Like the climate, a nation's economy is an incredibly complex thing made up of millions of discrete variables. But what makes economics even more complex than climatology is the fact that some of those variables — in fact, most of them — are the actions of individual people, each working to satisfy their own specialized desires and needs.

Just as Mao believed he could design China's agricultural systems, certain economic experts began to believe they could design the economy. In the free market, anyone could buy or sell anything for any price. It was chaos, anarchy! There was no oversight. There had to be a better way of allocating resources. And so economic central planning, best exemplified in communist countries such as the Soviet Union, was born.

Instead of leaving consumers and producers to their own devices, these planners, following in the footsteps of Marx and Engels, would assemble committees of the best minds in the country, who would then decide how much of any given commodity was needed, and for what price it should be sold. Quotas were issued for steel, food, and anything else the government deemed useful. If not enough people wanted to make the given product, they were forced to. If too much was produced, the overproducers were punished. Prices were fixed and not allowed to fluctuate unless by permission of the planning committee. In this way, it was hoped, efficiency could be achieved.

The results were a disaster. Shortages and surpluses were everywhere. Nobody could get what they wanted, when they wanted it, and goods were alternately piling up, unsold in warehouses, and becoming so scarce that people would have to wait days in lines just to obtain the simple necessities of life. Famines were common, as not enough food was produced to feed the population. Eventually, rulers of even the most dedicated communist countries were forced to relax control of the economy and allow markets to function again, albeit in a severely controlled manner.

What went wrong? Many were inclined to believe that the panels of experts were just not smart enough, that the wrong men had been chosen, that the government would do better next time. But next time, the results were always the same. The powers that be couldn't see the fundamental flaw in their thought process. They reasoned that a plan must be better than no plan, without realizing that "no plan" was not actually what capitalism entailed. A free market economy doesn't depend on "no plan," but rather, millions of plans. It relies on the individual plans of every citizen, each calculated and recalculated to meet changing circumstances, infinitely flexible, and highly responsive to even slight changes in variables. All of these plans intersected like a jigsaw puzzle to create a functioning economy that was self-correcting. If the price of a commodity goes up, people buy less of it and switch to other substitutes. Producers respond by producing more of the products that are in demand and less of those people aren't buying. There's constant feedback between buyer and seller, as they exchange information far more rapidly than any one mind can keep up with.

The price system alone is a miracle of communication. When you see a sticker price on something at the grocery store, that one number contains an aggregate of millions of bits of information that went into the item's production, as well as information about environmental conditions and consumer demand. The price of oranges reflects the weather patterns in Florida and California, the demand for juice, nutritionists' advice about the effects of sugar on children, demand for substitutes like apples, the costs of gasoline and other shipping expenses, and a thousand other variables. The consumer doesn't need to know all this to make an informed decision about what to purchase. All he has to do is look at the sticker price. It's simple, elegant, beautiful, and extremely effective. For an assembled committee of experts, no matter how brainy, to attempt to replicate artificially what the price conveys naturally is an exercise in futility.

Chief among the opponents of the central planning model were two economists from Austria (Austria again! Seeing a pattern?) Ludwig von Mises wrote a scathing treatise called *Socialism*, explaining in at times tedious detail that, without naturally occurring prices, bureaucrats had no ability to know how resources should be allocated. It was impossible to decide how many nails to make without knowing the price of iron. Once that basic signaling system broke down, calculation of any kind became impossible. Mises called this the economic calculation problem under socialism, and his argument today remains unanswerable, even by the staunchest advocates of modern socialism. That's why socialist economies today (with the exception of North Korea, which remains a basket case outlier) practice a form of market socialism, in which market prices are still allowed to prevail in an otherwise centrally-planned system.

The contributions of Mises to economic theory cannot be overstated, but perhaps the most dogged opponent of central planning was his compatriot, F.A. Hayek, still another Austrian economist, albeit with a slightly different view of markets than Mises and Menger had.

Hayek was obsessed with the organic nature of human society, and how highly functional systems seemed to arise out of thin air. Nobody consciously designs our interactions with one another, and yet in areas like the economic sphere, things just seem to magically work out. Adam Smith referred to this phenomenon as the Invisible Hand of the marketplace, a mysterious metaphysical force that directs activity towards a harmonious whole. Hayek built on this idea, coining the term "spontaneous order."

Have you ever watched a flock of geese migrating south for the winter? Have you noticed how they form an almost perfect V shape in the sky? Although the pattern is orderly, there is no chief goose who planned out the pattern and instructs each goose on what to do in order to achieve it. The V emerges naturally from each individual animal doing what makes the most sense for itself. The resulting pattern is an accident, but a beautiful one. This is an example of spontaneous order, a phenomenon that is responsible for a surprising amount of human activity.

Jimmy Wales, the founder of Wikipedia, read Hayek and was inspired by his ideas. At that time, encyclopedias were bulky, expensive, and took years to produce. Companies would assemble vast armies of experts, pay them to write articles, subject them to rigorous editing and fact-checking, format and print the text in handsome volumes that took up entire shelves, and sold them for thousands of dollars. Mostly, people didn't buy them. Jimmy Wales saw a way to do it differently. He wanted to harvest the wisdom of crowds and employ spontaneous order to distribute knowledge all over the world. So he started a website and allowed anyone to edit it. Before long, he had collected a body of knowledge that far exceeded the wildest dreams of even the most ambitious encyclopedist. And it was completely free.

For a long time, people laughed at Wikipedia, dismissed it as unreliable and foolish. But after an academic study confirmed that, on average, Wikipedia is just as accurate as print encyclopedias like the Encyclopedia Britannica, people became forced to take it seriously.[21] Now, it's the go-to source for information about absolutely anything.

How is this possible? How can a constantly-changing website be reliable when any Joe Shmoe off the street can edit it at any time? The beauty and functionality of Wikipedia works in the same way as the price system, thousands of instantaneous interactions working to self-correct. The fact checking and editing takes place

---

21 "Wikipedia Survives Research Test," *BBC News*, December 15, 2005.

in real time, all the time, by unpaid volunteers who do it purely for the love of the work. If someone tries to put up something untrue, unconfirmed, or improperly cited, it gets taken down almost immediately. The watchful eyes of thousands of editors keep each other in check, so that no one point of view can gain a foothold as fact without overwhelming amounts of supporting evidence. No one thought it could work, but it does. And not only does it work, but it works far better than anything that came before. All of us, as it turns out, are smarter than any of us.

Writing about his profession, Hayek once commented, "The curious task of economics is to demonstrate to men how little they know about what they imagine they can design." His point was that, like the now-unemployed encyclopedist of yesteryear, social planners simply lack the capacity to know as much as the accumulated information latent in the economy. No one can hope to outperform the multitudes; a million heads are better than one. Hayek called this "The Knowledge Problem."

When a Wired magazine editor coined the term "crowdsourcing" in 2006, he probably didn't realize he was reacting to spontaneous order in action facilitated by the internet's ability to bring people together from all over the world. Today, crowdsourcing, crowdfunding, and other forms of decentralized action are emerging as paradigm-changing revolutions, all of which could have been predicted by Hayek, but which eluded the majority of the world's most educated economists at the time. In fact, this idea continues to elude them even now.

Is Economics a Science?

Hayek's economic insight was not limited to recognizing how order can arise without a central plan. He also pinpointed the major error in the scientific community in trying to apply methods from the natural sciences to human society. Science is a wonderful tool for uncovering knowledge, but it has its limits, notably the fact that the scientific method, the methodology that has rightfully earned science its reputation as a tool for discovering truth, cannot be applied in all cases.

What is the scientific method exactly? Too many people who demand unquestioning obedience and fealty to the men in white coats don't really understand what it means, but it's actually quite simple. Science works in a number of steps. Applied one after another, these steps have been able to solve mysteries that eluded even the most brilliant rational minds throughout the ages.

To practice the scientific method, simply do the following:

1. Make an observation.
2. Propose a hypothesis.
3. Conduct an experiment to confirm or disprove the hypothesis.
4. Repeat.

A famous example involves Galileo and the Leaning Tower of Pisa. Observing objects falling, Galileo began to wonder what determines their rate of descent. Until that time, it had been accepted fact that heavier objects would fall faster than lighter ones. Galileo wasn't so sure about this, so he formulated the hypothesis that objects of different weights would fall at the same rate. He then had to test this hypothesis, so he went up to the top of the Tower of

Pisa, and dropped two weights over the side, measuring the amount of time each took to hit the ground. It turns out he was right. While air resistance can keep lighter objects like feathers airborne for a long time, gravity itself has nothing to do with weight or mass. Two objects of different masses do fall at the same rate, and Galileo's hypothesis was confirmed.

This works great in the natural sciences. Chemists, physicists, geologists, biologists, and so on use this technique all the time, and with amazing results. But not all experiments are as simple as the one Galileo performed four hundred years ago. How do you test more complicated propositions like, for example, "Do tougher gun laws reduce gun violence?" The knee-jerk reaction is that such a test would be simple. Look at places with tougher gun laws and compare their rates of gun crime to elsewhere. Easy, right? Not so fast.

One of the key principles of statistical analysis is that, to get meaningful results, you have to change only one variable at a time. Chicago has tougher gun laws than Kansas City, and also higher rates of gun violence. From that, we could conclude that tougher gun laws don't work, right? But wait a minute: France has tougher gun laws than the United States, and lower rates of gun crime. So that means gun laws *do* work to reduce violence, right? The problem is obvious. Kansas City and Chicago have lots of differences apart from gun laws. The United States and France have even more differences. How do we know that the difference in crime rates is explained by the legal structure and not by one of these other variables?

Statisticians have ways of trying to account for and correct for these additional variables, but the fact is that you can't perform a controlled experiment in a human society in the same way you can in a physics lab. Even if you account for every other variable, there's still the unpredictability of human behavior that always throws a wrench in the works.

In his book The *Counter-Revolution in Science*, Hayek pointed out that it's inappropriate to apply the methods of physical science to human society for the simple reason that humans behave differently than inanimate objects. You can roll a ball down a ramp a hundred times, and as long as you keep force, direction, temperature, friction, and any other relevant variables constant, it will behave in exactly the same way every time. Put a hundred people in the same situation, or one person in a situation a hundred times, and you will get a multitude of unpredictable reactions. This is because humans act with purpose to try to achieve goals, using their free will to make decisions in ways that balls on ramps can't. And while many scientists believe that free will is an illusion and that behavior would ultimately be predictable if we could account for every biological and environmental factor in a person's life, as yet this task has proved far too daunting for even the most advanced computers.

The upshot of this is that economics can't make reliable predictions about human society — the tools are simply not appropriate to the task. This is why economists have earned a reputation alongside weathermen as horrible forecasters. They never know when the next recession is going to come, they can't predict what inflation or unemployment is going to be next month, and they can't tell you how much revenue a tax increase will bring in. The reason is that all these calculations require second-guessing how people are going to react. No economist, however well-educated, can know ahead of time if people are going to decide *en masse* to sell off their stock holdings, or to what extent workers will modify their behavior to avoid getting hit with a tax increase. Even John Maynard

Keynes, one of the major advocates for government intervening in the economy to "correct" the market process, effectively threw up his hands in defeat when asked to explain how recessions happen. He blamed "the animal spirits," irrational urges that seize the population like a mass delusion and result in financial collapses. Actually, Hayek won a Nobel Prize for his work on explaining exactly why recessions happen, and what can be done to prevent them, but that is a story for another book, or at least another chapter.

Behavioral Economics

After World War II, the progressive movement didn't really go away, it just went underground for a while. While words like "eugenics" are no longer fashionable, the concept of using science, directed by those at the top of the food chain, of course, to improve society is still very much in vogue in certain academic circles, unable to let go of the idea that their superior brains endow them with the wisdom to plan and direct all of the other mindless sheep who make up the bulk of the country.

These days, the progressive movement has a large presence in what has been termed the field of "behavioral economics.". The basic idea is to use the tools of economics — money, prices, and advertising, psychology, etc. — to influence people's behavior in ways that will be "socially beneficial." Apologies for all the scare quotes, but when dealing with the sorts of people who find behavioral economics attractive, euphemism and Orwellian Newspeak is so common that it becomes challenging to use ordinary words and phrases without qualification.

The basic theory goes something like this: people are idiots who engage in behaviors that are not only personally destructive, but bad for society as a whole. It is therefore the responsibility of all of us (read: government) to correct these behaviors. But since the Constitution generally forbids using direct force on people who are minding their own business, it has to be done covertly, in such a way that most people don't even realize they are being controlled.

Practically, this can be done in a variety of ways. Some are fairly innocuous, like the physical arrangement of items in stores. Psychologists have discovered that people are more likely to buy products located at eye level, so behavioral economists argue for using this knowledge to put healthier, more environmentally friendly items there, while placing more socially costly items in harder to reach places, thereby encouraging people to "shop responsibly." This is a little manipulative, but not exactly the end of the world. After all, you have to make decisions when designing a store; the merchandise has to go somewhere, so why not put it where it will do the most good?

But when these seemingly harmless choices, taken with the deliberate goal of modifying behavior, pile up, they start to get a little creepy. In the book *Nudge* by former Obama administration official Cass Sunstein and behavioral economist Richard Thaler, the authors argue for what they call "libertarian paternalism." (In my view, a contradiction in terms). Recognizing that they can't mandate that children eat more fruit, they argue that we can instead require schools to present fruit at the front of the cafeteria line, where it is more likely to be eaten. Lamenting that we can't force people to donate their organs after they die, they want to explicitly ask people if they want to join the organ donor registry, knowing that those who are put on the spot are more likely to say yes.[22] A lot of these nudges involve requiring people to opt out of things, rather than opt in, because most people won't bother to take the time and effort to do so.

This kind of thinking has always made me uncomfortable. I prefer to let people make their own choices without even the subtle nudges Sunstein and Thaler are advocating for. It seems dishonest to deliberately manipulate the masses into behavior that some cabal of officials thinks is desirable.

In my youth, I spent a year working in a record store. I have always loved music, and this had been a lifelong dream of mine, albeit a small one. The work was fun and the environment a pleasant one, but there was one thing that bothered me: the marketing department. We would have large bins full of budget CDs that sold for five dollars each. However, the stickers on the CDs did not say "$5" as one might expect, but rather "2 for $10". Most people would assume that, in order to get the low price, you had to buy two CDs, and would do so. We didn't lie to anyone. If they asked, we would happily tell them that the deal applied to single CDs as well. But nevertheless, the reason for labeling the product in this way was to deliberately mislead people into spending more money than they otherwise would. When the store finally went out of business, a huge banner was placed out front reading "Going out of business! 50% off!" I would then have the pleasure of fending off the angry and frustrated customers who had missed the "on select items" tag printed in type so small you'd have to have eyes like a

---

22 Benjamin Wallace-Wells, "Cass Sunstein Wants to Nudge Us", *New York Times*, May 13, 2010.

fighter pilot to notice it.

I get it. It's the marketing department's job to earn money for the store, but it always felt sleazy and dishonest to me, so much so that I would deliberately tell customers the information marketing was trying to hide. Fortunately, the market has a way of punishing this kind of behavior if customers don't like it. As I mentioned, that record store is no longer in business.

When the marketing department belongs to government, however, customers have nowhere else to go if they don't like being manipulated. There is no competition, and no ability to withhold money from the tax collectors, at least as long as you want to stay out of jail.

For a while, I participated in a group of economists specializing in savings and retirement policy. It's a fairly interesting area of policy, with some significant real-world problems that need to be solved. But I stopped participating, largely because the focus of most meetings was a group of Washington experts debating how we could trick people into saving a higher fraction of their earnings. Of course, they didn't use the word "trick." Economists prefer to say "incentivize." I always wondered how these people knew enough about American workers to decide how much each person ought to save. They didn't know the individual circumstances of these people's lives. Maybe they had a good reason for refraining from saving. Maybe they have sick relatives with big medical bills, or are embarking on an entrepreneurial venture that requires a big investment up front, but promises to pay dividends in the future. Maybe they only have six months to live, and see no point in saving for a future they won't ever see. None of this was ever considered. The assumption was that workers were just irresponsible and short-sighted. But so what if they are? It's not the job of government to tell people how much they should value money tomorrow versus money today. A person's retirement should be his own business, but when economists get involved, nobody is ever just left in peace to make their own decisions.

Our Bean Counters, Our Masters

As Hayek said, the curious task of economics is to demonstrate to men how little they really know about what they imagine they can design. But you'd never know it from talking to economists today. They seem to think that the task of economics is to tell people how to live their lives using data as the pretense of scientific objectivity. Having studied statistics and econometrics extensively in graduate school, let me be the first to tell you, data is anything but objective.

The more you learn about statistical methodology, the more you realize how easy it is to manipulate the results to suit whatever theory the researchers started out with. I'm not talking about academic fraud. This is standard operating procedure among data scientists. Computer programs are used to run regressions — the equations that determine correlations between variables — in many different ways, yielding many different results. And since only studies with statistically significant results get published, economists are biased towards some interpretations of the data over others. Most of the time, they don't even realize they're doing it.

Because economists want us to believe, and generally believe themselves, that their policy recommendations are coming from science rather than mere opinion, it becomes easy to justify the use of force to control the population. At its worst, this can look like the eugenics movement in the early 20th century. At its best, it looks like Cass Sunstein's version of libertarian paternalism, in which we are all nudged towards the preferred outcome of some economist overlord.

The Austrian School of economics pushed back against this kind of thinking, arguing instead for individual choice, the wisdom of crowds, spontaneous order, and the beautiful but messy chaos of human society. Perhaps it's no coincidence that, despite Nobel Prizes and more than a century of correct predictions, the Austrians have continued to be kept firmly out of the mainstream.

PART THREE
Medicine

We all dread going to the doctor. Part of it is the fear that he may discover something amiss in our anatomy, that we may be dying and that, if only we hadn't asked someone to look into it, we might have been able to go on living in blissful ignorance. Hey, no one ever said the human race was logical. Part of it is the pure discomfort, the embarrassment of allowing another person to grope, fondle and inspect your most intimate body parts. Part of it, to be sure, is the expense.

But there is another reason we hate going to the doctor, one that only makes sense if we understand how the traditional servant-master relationship gets turned on its head. We fear going to the doctor, because we don't want to be in trouble. We don't want to disappoint the authority figure. We want his approval. We don't want him to frown and scold us for eating too much and exercising too little. We don't want to hear his thoughts on tobacco and alcohol; they make us feel guilty. It's the same feeling we get when coming home to show mommy and daddy a bad report card. We don't want that feeling of shame and guilt.

way. Like teachers, we employ doctors to perform a service for us. They work on our behalf to represent our interests. We are the customers, and if the customer isn't happy, he can simply take his money and go home. Doctors should bend over backwards to try to keep us happy, and we should know that if we lie to them — which we all do — then we're only cheating ourselves. This is so universally true that the popular medical drama *House* made a mantra out of the phrase "everybody lies," taking it for granted that patients would try to hide embarrassing truths from their doctors even when it could cost them their lives. We can dismiss this behavior as irrational, but it explains a lot more if we assume that deep down, most people *don't* regard doctors as their advocates as much as their adversaries.

When reason conflicts with experience, one of the two must be wrong and usually, sad to say, it is reason which must yield to reality. The truth is that we fear doctors because they are really not our servants at all. For years, the medical profession as a whole has been gradually assuming greater and greater degrees of control over the people it is supposed to be helping.

Munchausen Syndrome by Proxy

In medicine, it is well known that certain people seek attention from doctors and family members by feigning illness and manufacturing imaginary symptoms. This used to be called "malingering." Today, in the continuing war against perfectly decent English words, doctors call it Munchausen Syndrome, named after the literary character Baron Munchausen, known for telling wildly exaggerated stories about himself.

We'll return to malingerers later in this section, but there is another form of this disorder called Munchausen Syndrome by proxy, or MSP.

According to WebMD, MSP is "a psychological disorder marked by attention-seeking behavior by a caregiver through those who are in their care."

The article goes on to say, "People with MSP may create or exaggerate a child's symptoms in several ways. They may simply lie about symptoms, alter tests (such as contaminating a urine sample), falsify medical records, or they may actually induce symptoms through various means, such as poisoning, suffocating, starving, and causing infection."

You may remember a particularly chilling scene in the film *The Sixth Sense* in which a mother mixes rat poison into her daughter's soup in order to keep the girl sick and dependent on the mother as a caregiver. This is Munchausen Syndrome by proxy. It's especially disturbing because of the betrayal of trust involved, in which a person expected to be the supreme caregiver and advocate for the patient, the mother, reverses roles and engages in actively hostile behavior.

WebMD regards MSP as a very rare mental disorder, but in fact this kind of mentality — the desire to secretly worsen a problem in order to keep devoting oneself to it — is quite common, albeit in a milder and more subtle form.

After You, My Dear Munchausen

Shirley Jackson was an American author most famous for her horror-themed short story, *The Lottery,* in which a small town engages in human sacrifice to ensure peace, prosperity, and a good harvest. The sacrifice of the individual for the good of the collective could just as easily serve as a running theme throughout this book, but another of her stories, less frequently remembered but especially powerful for me, serves as a perfect illustration of what I am trying to get at.

The story *After You, My Dear Alphonse,* is a seemingly innocuous slice of American life, centering around two young boys, Johnny and Boyd, who come in for lunch after a morning of rigorous play. Johnny's mother, a kindly, sympathetic woman, serves them sandwiches and makes conversation with her son's young friend, who happens to be black.

The mother extends one generous offer after another to the boy and his family. First she asks if he wants to take any leftover food home with him, then offers him some of Johnny's hand-me-down clothing. Each time Boyd refuses. His responses are polite, but filled with confusion. His father is the foreman of a factory. His mother doesn't work. They make good money. They can buy anything they need. When Boyd needs new clothes, they rely on a department store, not someone else's cast offs. Eventually, the mother becomes angry with Boyd's apparent lack of gratitude and storms off. Distressed, Boyd turns to Johnny and asks what he did wrong. Johnny shrugs and dismisses his mother's behavior as crazy, at which point they both go out to play again. End of story.

Like most of Jackson's stories, this one has a subtlety that is more powerful than any overt anti-racism message ever could be. Johnny's mother assumes Boyd's family is poor because they are black, and relishes the opportunity to demonstrate her own charity. When it turns out that she is mistaken, that her charity is unnecessary, she bristles. Like Boyd, the readers are left to interpret and explain her reaction on their own.

In normal circumstances, one would expect the success of a neighbor to be something worth celebrating. Even if we can't be happy for them in a purely empathetic way, surely the fact they they no longer need our charity, charity which necessarily imposes a cost on the givers, should be a welcome relief of responsibility. The fact that we so often observe the opposite reaction speaks volumes about the human condition.

Offering to help someone is an implicit statement of superiority. If they need help, and you can give it, that means you are in some way better than them. And if the person receiving the help can't do without it, so much the better. It makes you feel important and needed, while it makes them dependent on you, puts them in your debt, and ultimately in your power. The recipient of aid becomes like the children who, living under your roof, have to follow your rules.

None of this is to say that it's bad to be charitable, but it is bad to use charity as a means of controlling other people, either directly or indirectly. In the story, one could argue that Johnny's mother is suffering from a mild form of Munchausen's Syndrome by proxy, in which she tries to use a young boy's perceived weakness as a means of making herself feel more important. When her efforts are frustrated, she gets angry. While Johnny's mother is a fictional character, you've probably known people like this in real life as well. I know I have.

In the Bible, Jesus warns about the do-gooder who wears his virtues on his sleeve. Real virtue, he argues, is not done for recognition or glory, but because it is simply the right thing to do. The same goes for people who act charitably only when people are watching, and who care more about their own aggrandizement than in actually helping people.

First, Do No Harm

It may seem strange to single out the medical profession as an instrument of social control. Ostensibly, the sole duty of doctors is to treat patients and keep them healthy and alive. Without health and life, we can hardly be free to live up to our full potential, so what could possibly be wrong with the people dedicated to preserving those qualities?

Part of the problem is the exclusivity of the medical profession itself, in regards to who is allowed to offer treatment, what types of treatment they are allowed to offer, what kind of equipment they are allowed to use, and what sorts of payment they are allowed to receive.

The American Medical Association (AMA) exercises very tight control over who can practice medicine or attend medical school. Medical schools have quotas and limits to the number of applicants they accept each year. The requirements to receive a medical license are extremely strict, expensive, and time-consuming. And qualified physicians emigrating from other countries are generally not allowed to practice in the United States without having to redo most or all of their training, a luxury for which most people have neither the time nor money.

Why would an association dedicated to medicine deliberately limit the number of people who can become doctors, who could potentially save lives and increase the quality of life for patients everywhere? The short answer is that, like it or not, medicine is a business like any other. As noble as the motives of many doctors might be, they are ultimately out to make a profit, and one of the worst things for a business' bottom line is competition. Every new doctor who gets licensed threatens to take away patients from established doctors. And the people who do the decision-making at the AMA tend to be, you guessed it, established doctors.

It sounds cynical, but it happens in every profession, not just medicine. In the United States, about a third of all occupations now require some kind of license for practitioners.[23] This is up from just 5 percent 50 years ago. The reason for this is not safety or consumer

23 Brad Hershbein, David Boddy, & Melissa S. Kearney, "Nearly 30 Percent of Workers in the U.S. Need a License to Perform Their Job," *Brookings Institute*, January 27, 2015.

protection, but the influence of lobbyists trying to crack down on unfettered competition. Hairdressers, florists, interior decorators, hypnotists, and a host of other occupations can't be done without a license, not because the public needs to be protected from bad haircuts, but because established barbers don't like putting up with young upstarts threatening their business.

The principle is the same with medicine. Of course, undergoing surgery carries more of a risk for consumers than buying a dozen roses, but there are plenty of medical procedures that people with a minimum of medical training could easily perform without having to undergo eight years of medical school and tens of thousands of dollars in training expenses. Setting a broken arm or prescribing penicillin for an infection is not exactly rocket science, and yet we are forbidden from buying these services from anyone except a select few, approved by the AMA and, by extension, by our government.

A shortage of doctors means a couple of things for the population at large. First, it means we pay higher prices. It's a simple law of supply and demand that the fewer sellers there are, the more they can afford to charge. We all have a reflexive hatred of monopolies, not least because of the years of childhood trauma suffered at the feet of the eponymous board game, but the artificial reduction of supply in something like the medical oligopoly, for whatever reason, arouses less suspicion.

The second implication of the AMA's restrictions is that we have fewer choices in the sort of doctors we want to use. In addition to the sheer numbers of doctors being smaller than they might otherwise be, the universal standards imposed on doctors and hospitals mean that the very types of medicine we are allowed to purchase remain unnecessarily limited.

The argument for this system has always been one of safety. Medicine is a dangerous profession requiring a huge amount of specialized knowledge, and so the government needs to ensure that the general public is protected from charlatans, con artists, and the incompetent. It's a persuasive case until you realize that giving a central authority the power to decide what constitutes "good" medicine takes the power of choice out of the hands, not only of patients, but of doctors themselves.

Suppose that you have a rare, life-threatening disease. Your doctor tells you that traditional medicines have little chance of saving your life, but that there are experimental treatments that might work. The problem is, these treatments have not been approved for use by the Food and Drug Administration, the organization responsible for approving drugs and medical devices for use. In the name of keeping people safe, the government prevents you from pursuing options that may save your life. The perversity of this way of thinking is clear.

Thankfully, situations such as the one above are common enough that people have begun to take notice. After a protracted campaign by patients' rights advocates, most states passed so-called Right to Try laws — laws which allow terminal patients to try experimental drugs under certain circumstances. And in 2018, President Trump signed a federal bill into law to establish Right to Try nationwide.[24] Good, but far too late, and not nearly enough. Right to Try still requires a huge amount of bureaucracy for patients to get the treatments they want, including lengthy delays that could cost lives. It is not as simple as a patient and doctor simply agreeing on

24 Allie Malloy, "Trump Signs 'Right to Try' Act Aiming at Helping Terminally Ill Patients Seek Drug Treatments," *CNN*, May 30, 2018.

a treatment and pursuing it. The FDA still has to be involved, in a far too invasive way. Nevertheless, progress is progress, and should be celebrated as such.

The terminally ill are not the only ones who could benefit from more medical choice. State of the art treatments are amazing for those who can afford them, but some people don't have that kind of money, and disease doesn't discriminate based on wealth.

If you need a car, but don't have a ton of cash, you can buy a used Honda rather than a brand-new Lamborghini. If you're hungry, you can buy canned beans instead of lobster. But the medical equivalent of Hondas and beans are not only inferior, but outlawed. Patients are forbidden from pursuing lower-cost medical options, even if they are the only ones they can afford. Again, the rationalization has to do with safety, but surely less-than-perfect treatments that patients can afford are safer than no treatments at all.

It is for this reason that I regard the FDA as the most dangerous of all government agencies. It literally forces innocent American citizens to die by forbidding that they use certain drugs and medical devices that could cure them. The sick and the poor have few enough options already without the FDA further restricting them.

This does not just apply to pharmaceuticals. Many people are skeptical of Western medicine and prefer to pursue alternative treatments. Some have allergic reactions to key drugs like penicillin that make alternatives less of an option and more of a necessity. I am personally not a believer in alternative medicines like homeopathy, acupuncture, or chiropractic, but there are millions of people who swear that such treatments give them relief. I would not wish to deprive them of their preferred course of treatment, especially given the very poor track record of Western medicine, which until quite recently engaged in practices that we now know to be laughably ineffective or even harmful.

Only a century ago, doctors were still extracting blood with leeches in the hopes of magically curing various ailments. Only two centuries ago, no doctor ever considered washing his hands before surgery, resulting in infections that needlessly killed countless patients. For all our advances, the human body still remains largely mysterious, and it is hubris to think that Western doctors are always right and alternatives are always wrong. Why not give the patient a chance to make up his own mind? The slogan "my body, my choice" need not apply to only one thing.

To give a particularly recent example, the benefits of medical cannabis are now finally being recognized. Used as a folk remedy for centuries, cannabis became demonized as a dangerous and addictive drug as the combined result of DuPont pharmaceuticals wanting tighter control of the market, the newspaper magnate William Randolph Hearst's desire to crush hemp as a competitor to newsprint, and prejudice against Mexicans and the "degenerate races".[25] As if most of the drugs doctors give patients today aren't dangerous or addictive. One need only watch any pharmaceutical commercial on television to see that about half the ad is dedicated to a rapid-fire list of dangers that could imperil the incautious patient. Medicine is dangerous by nature, and it is disingenuous for regulators to persecute one drug while handing out other equally dangerous ones like candy.

Fortunately, a majority of states have now legalized medical cannabis, and federal involvement in enforcing laws against the

---

25 David McDonald, "The Racist Roots of Marijuana Prohibition," *Foundation for Economic Education*, April 11, 2017.

plant seem to be on the way out. This is good news for thousands of patients across the country, but only a small victory in a wider fight for patient choice.

The consequences of preventing patients from getting the treatments they want is that they either go without or they go elsewhere. Defenders of abortion constantly warn us of the dangers of back-alley, coat-hanger operations that forego hygiene and put the life of the mother at risk. The same principle applies to all medicine. If people can't get it legally, they will get it illegally, and illegal medicine is usually a one-way ticket to the morgue.

Medical tourism, in which patients unable to get care in the U.S. either because they can't afford it or it is outlawed, travel to Mexico or other countries with lax medical regulations in a desperate attempt to find someone, anyone, who will help them. In 2016, an estimated 1.4 million Americans traveled abroad for the purpose of getting medical treatment, participating in a $439 billion medical tourism industry.[26]

If people are going to purchase back-alley medicine anyway, wouldn't it be better if they could do so from the comfort of their own homes? If people can't afford Ferraris and lobster, shouldn't they be allowed to buy Hondas and beans? And yet when most people talk about medical tourism, they're referring, not to low-budget Mexican surgeons, but to taking advantage of the allegedly generous universal health care systems of countries like Canada, France, and the United Kingdom, systems that are believed to be better because they are run by the government, which brings us nicely to...

---

26 Beth Braverman, "1.4 Million Americans Will Go Abroad for Medical Care This Year. Should You?" *The Fiscal Times*, August 17, 2016.

The Myth of Free Health Care

There ain't no such thing as a free lunch. This was the catchphrase popularized by science fiction writer Robert Heinlein in his novel *The Moon Is a Harsh Mistress*, and further used by free market economist Milton Friedman. It derives from a (probably apocryphal) anecdote about a diner advertising free lunches, only for the hungry patrons to find that they were forced to listen to an advertising spiel before they could eat. One disgruntled customer allegedly muttered on his way out of the building, "There ain't no such thing as a free lunch."

Apocryphal or not, the story illustrates a deeper truth, which is that nothing comes without a cost of some kind. It may not be monetary, but rest assured, sooner or later you're going to pay. This is especially true with the market for health care. It has become fashionable for the smart set to argue, with tears of compassion in their eyes, that medicine is far too important to be a business, that health care is in fact an inalienable human right. Only a selfish monster, after all, would charge somebody to save their life, or would refuse to save a life because of lack of sufficient funds to pay. Health care, we are told, must be free and available to all. It's the only way we can consider ourselves a civilized people.

This all sounds very nice, and it must be admitted that it would be lovely if everyone could receive life-saving medical attention for free, just as it would be lovely if we could add two plus two and get a hundred. But life simply does not work that way.

There is a cost to everything, and few things more so than becoming a qualified doctor. The training lasts more than a decade and generally runs into the hundreds of thousands of dollars. That doesn't include malpractice insurance, staffing costs, equipment, rent for the practice, taxes, complying with medical records regulations, keeping up with medical literature, attending conferences, and all the other expenses involved in being a practicing physician. In short, being a doctor is very, very, very expensive.

Are we really supposed to ask such people to give away their services for nothing? Should they work from dawn to dusk, seven days a week, like slaves, with no compensation for their efforts whatsoever, just because they chose to go to medical school instead of, say, law school? Obviously not. If we expected this of doctors, almost no one would bother to become one, and far more lives would be cost in doctor shortages than would be saved by the few altruists out there.

Actually, in spite of the fear mongering you hear about uninsured patients dying in gutters, most emergency rooms will not turn away patients for an inability to pay. Free clinics exist, and rare indeed would be the doctor who would not lend his skill to a poor person on death's door. The Hippocratic Oath, in its modern version administered by the AMA, demands that doctors act with compassion and empathy, and not neglect their obligations to their fellow man. The cartoon image of a callous doctor who won't perform the Heimlich Maneuver until a patient's check has cleared is not a reflection of reality. Still, professional ethics aside, it is unreasonable to expect that doctors should receive no compensation for their years of study and numerous operating expenses.

If we think it's fair for doctors to get paid for the work they do, just like everyone else, the obvious next question becomes "Who pays them?" In most fields, customers pay prices in exchange for goods and services that they want or need. You want a car? You pay the dealership. You want a house? You pay the realtor. Don't want either of these things? No problem. Keep your money to use on something else.

As simple as it is, this turns out to be a pretty good system for a variety of reasons. Keeping payments between sellers and customers promotes accountability and choice. The buyer has an incentive to shop around and get a good value, because it's his own money he's using, but at the same time he doesn't want to sacrifice too much quality, because he is ultimately the one who has to live with the product. The seller has an incentive to be competent and honest, because if the people who purchase his services are unhappy, word will get out and he will possibly be driven out of business, or at least forced to reduce his prices. Moreover, the buyer can choose to withhold his money at any time, and take it to the competition instead. This relationship between buyer and seller keeps both parties honest.

There are some goods, however, that people consider so fundamentally important that everyone should have them, regardless of their ability to pay. Not being able to afford medicine, like not being able to afford food, is a death sentence for many people. Rather than let these people die in the streets, it is argued that someone else must pay on their behalf.

This argument, as far as it goes, is a pretty good one. No one wants poor people dying of easily preventable diseases or easily treatable injuries. To ignore their plight would be heartless. As far as I know, there is no disagreement on this point, despite certain caricatures of the cold-hearted libertarian who wants all the poor to die in disease-ridden ghettos. Where disagreement does occur is over the best way to help the poor get the care they need.

Conventional wisdom holds that man is a selfish and greedy animal, unwilling to come to the aid of his brothers and sisters in all but the most remarkable of circumstances. It is this callousness, the bureaucrats and politicians argue, that necessitates the intervention of government. The implication, of course, is that elected officials and their hired lackeys are cut from a finer cloth than the rest of us, and while we, the voters, would happily let vagrants bleed to death on our doorsteps, the noble public servants really care.

I hope that none of my readers is naïve enough to swallow the notion that the Members of Congress are morally better than the rest of us, a notion that is disproved every day in the headlines of a thousand papers revealing sordid tales of vice, corruption, and dishonesty in the halls of the Capitol building. But even if you do ascribe noble motives to those creatures that scurry and skulk from legislative hearings to smoke-filled back rooms, the solutions they propose are deeply problematic.

Know Your Rights

It is all well and good to point out that medical school is expensive and that doctors deserve to be paid, but what about what the patients deserve? Don't they have a right to health care? The concept of rights is a particularly sticky one, because it means so many different things to so many different people. There is a difference between legal rights and moral rights, between negative rights and positive rights. Most people don't think about these differences and merely declare that they have a right to anything that seems good or important.

Asserting a right to health care is easy populism, but actually solves nothing, raising far more questions than it answers, the first of which is "How much health care?" There is no one good called "health care" that you can either have or not have. Health encompasses everything from a Band-Aid to brain surgery and heart transplants. Does everyone have the right to the best, state-of-the-art surgery money can buy? Or is the right restricted to some more basic, but necessarily arbitrary level? Does everyone have the right to an MRI or CT Scan? Does everyone have the right to morphine or Viagra? Does everyone have the right to be operated on by the most skilled surgeons, or will lesser doctors suffice? Does everyone have the right to an unlimited stay in a hospital, complete with meals and attending nurses, free of charge? Once you start asking these types of questions, it's easy to see why the idea of a right to health care is a tricky one.

The right to health care is what's known in ethics as a "positive right". Unlike negative rights, positive rights require other people to take some action. The right to free speech is a negative right. No one needs to do anything for that right to remain intact. They just have to refrain from interfering with speech. By contrast, a positive right requires constant and active effort in order to be upheld. If I have a right to as much health care as I want or need, then by implication I am making a claim on the time and resources of doctors, nurses, technicians, and administrators, who must attend to me or else deny me my rights. Positive rights run into logical difficulties, because they raise practical questions that cannot easily be answered. What if there are more sick people than there are doctors? How do we decide whose rights to violate? What about poor countries where there is no advanced medicine? Is every member of the population therefore being denied a human right merely by virtue of where he lives?

The alleged right to medicine is not a real argument, so much as it is a talking point designed to persuade the public to give ever more power to the government so that it can control and regulate the medical profession. The irony is that, as we shall see, these controls and regulations are almost always bad for the patients.

Physician, Insure Thyself

It would take many more words than I am willing to write here to unravel everything that is wrong with America's health care system, but let me at least attempt an explanation by tackling two of its most troubling components: health insurance, and the purportedly universal coverage of the Patient Protection and Affordable Care Act, more commonly known as ObamaCare.

Health insurance, like all the world's greatest evils, is pernicious because it masquerades so convincingly as good. The argument goes like this: sometimes bad things happen; we can't predict when those things will happen; so why not pay someone to take care of you if and when those bad things come crashing down on you all at once? Put simply, insurance is gambling. The policy holder is betting good money in the form of monthly premiums that something bad will happen soon, and the insurance company is betting that it won't. And like all good casinos, the house takes great pains to ensure that it always comes out on top.

For many individuals, particularly the unlucky ones, insurance can be a great deal, saving families from financial ruin, but the aggregate effect of insurance on health care markets is very bad indeed. Here's why: insurance breaks down that buyer-seller relationship discussed earlier by introducing a third-party payer into the transaction. Suddenly, the patient is not paying with his own money, meaning he has little reason to shop around for bargains, and doctors, observing that people with insurance don't seek out bargains, cease to see an upside in offering them. Add to this the fact that the AMA forbids advertising for most kinds of doctors, and you begin to see a little of the problem.

With no incentive to keep costs down, doctors allow their costs to go up, and up, and up. Sometimes, insurance companies are able to negotiate lower prices for themselves and their customers, but this does little good for people without insurance, who bear the full brunt of medical inflation.

It is this inflation that led to the mistaken idea that everyone must have insurance of some kind. Whereas it used to be common for doctors to make house calls and charge reasonable rates, which patients could pay out of pocket, today, everyone must be covered. Choosing to go uninsured would be financial, or even literal, suicide in the event of a health emergency, and as a civilized people, we cannot permit such irresponsibility on the part of American citizens. Enter the government, riding in on a shining white horse declaring that the days of pestilence and privation are over. Everyone will now have insurance coverage, for the simple reason that everyone will be legally required to have insurance coverage.

There is an old story about a small town that passed a law forbidding its residents to die, and imposing fines on the survivors of anyone who broke the law. The naysayers scoffed, of course, but lo and behold, after the law passed, death rates in the town began to plummet. Could this ridiculous legal mandate actually be saving lives? Well, no.

What actually happened was, fearful of incurring the legal fines associated with dying in town, family members of the sick and elderly transferred them to the next town over shortly before the expected end. People were still dying at the same rate, but the town created the illusion of longevity through a statistical trick.

This is very much like what has happened to health insurance under ObamaCare. It is true that the law increased insurance coverage. How could it not? Anyone who failed to purchase a policy would face stiff fines, set to escalate every year. Threaten people into buying insurance, and sure enough they do it. But what everyone seemed to overlook was the fact that insurance *per se* was never the goal. Health care, the ability to see doctors, receive diagnoses, fill prescriptions, get treatment, and ultimately get healthier and live longer; those were the real goals. In all the hubbub to get everyone insurance, lawmakers forgot why insurance was useful in the first place.

Earlier, I posed the somewhat rhetorical question, if doctors aren't supposed to work for free, who should pay them? Originally, patients paid them. Then, insurance companies paid them in place of the patients. Now, through a complex web of subsidies and mandates, the government does a large part of the paying, via the insurance companies, on behalf of the patients. In other words, a fourth-party payer has now been introduced, further weakening the relationship between patient and doctor, and further undermining the accountability and choice that makes markets work.

Under the insurance model, patients lost their incentive to search for good value for their money, but the insurance companies still needed to attract business by keeping premiums reasonable and actually paying for a procedure every now and again. But with the government mandate that everyone buy a policy, the incentive to compete for customers was gone. The American people were rounded up and handed to big insurers on a silver tray, ordered to pay whatever premiums were asked, or else face increasingly steep fines from the government. What more could any company want?

With a guaranteed customer base, insurers were free not only to raise premiums, but also to increase deductibles into the five-figure range, and restrict patients' ability to see local doctors or visit local hospitals at all. Having insurance isn't worth very much to a poor family if they have to pay a $10,000 deductible before they can use it. For many Americans, $10,000 might as well be $100,000. If you can't pay, you can't pay.

So while on paper, everyone has coverage, in reality, access to medicine remains a major problem. Universal health care turns out to be a fraud, something that serves as a great talking point for politicians, but which leaves actual patients out in the cold.

In the face of these skyrocketing costs, and with an inability to really lose customers, insurance companies have done what any profit-maximizing organization would be expected to do: tried to avoid paying out claims, using their own customers' behavior as an excuse.

Death Panels

What do you do if you're an insurance company, thinking about extending a policy to a man we'll call "Mr. Smith." You send an agent to meet with Mr. Smith, and discover that he is overweight, drinks heavily, smokes, doesn't exercise, has had three heart attacks already, and is 92 years old. Any sane company would either refuse to insure such a man, or else charge him astronomical premiums. However, the law prohibits you from discriminating based on age, as well as prohibiting you from denying coverage based on preexisting conditions (like three heart attacks).

The company can't refuse to insure Smith, but it can jack up his rates based on his behavior. Smoking and drinking are risky behaviors; the company can justify charging him more for engaging in them. This leaves Mr. Smith with a choice. He can either reform his behavior, or pay more money for insurance. He can't choose to go without insurance altogether; that would be against the law, remember. Supposing Mr. Smith is not a wealthy man, this decision is quickly reduced to no decision at all. The old man has to clean up his act, or else go to the poor house. Still worse, if Mr. Smith's insurance is subsidized by the government, Medicare for example, the insurers can refuse to pay for certain treatments on account of the cost and the high probability of death in a patient like Smith. Whether he technically has insurance coverage doesn't matter much if it won't pay the medical bills for his next, and final, heart attack.

Actions have consequences, and it is reasonable for insurance companies to charge more to customers who are likely to cost them more. What is not reasonable is to put people in a position where the government, via insurance mandates, can dictate how people live their lives.

In a free market, the person who wanted to behave irresponsibly would be free to do so, and if he got into trouble, it would be his own fault, and his own dime he would be spending getting himself out of it again. If a smoker gets emphysema or lung cancer, it is up to them to pay a doctor to treat them. The risk and the responsibility fall on the same person, so there is balance and an alignment of incentives.

On the other hand, when someone else is paying the bills, suddenly the rules change. "As long as you live under my roof, you'll play by my rules!" If government, or an insurance company, is paying for your medical treatments, they can then demand that you behave in ways that minimize their costs, such as refraining from drugs, healthy eating, and plenty of exercise.

In 2009, when the legislation that would become the Patient Protection and Affordable Care Act was taking shape, Gov. Sarah Palin and Rep. Michele Bachmann drew ridicule for their comments warning against the "death panels" that ObamaCare would create, should it become law. The phrase was dismissed as the unhinged ravings of two right-wing lunatics. One fact-checking website even went so far as to name the claim their "Lie of the Year."[27]

What the mainstream media failed to realize was that, election drama aside, they had a legitimate point, albeit hyperbolically made. Medicine, like everything else, is a scarce resource. There's only so much of it to go around, only so many doctors, only so many donor organs, only so many MRI machines. These resources have to be allocated in some way. The traditional way was to allocate them based on money. People who could pay for the most expensive procedures would get them. People who couldn't would get less expensive, and consequently less good, care.

This may seem unfair, but if you think about it, you'll realize that it's the same way everything else in society works. The point of money is to be able to afford better things, and better things tend to contribute to a longer life. The reason for this is that money is not distributed at random, but is a reflection of how much value is being created for other people. The only way to get money (without stealing it) is to do something that other people are willing to pay for. The people who do the most of this get rich, and rich people get

---

27 Angie Drobnic Holan, "PolitiFact's Lie of the Year: 'Death Panels,'" *PolitiFact*, December 19, 2009.

safer cars, healthier food, better police protection, better attorneys, cleaner environments, and personal trainers to keep them fit. All of these things contribute to greater health and longer life. Is there any reason to be morally outraged that they get better medicine as well? If they didn't, there would hardly be any point in trying to become rich in the first place.

The alternative to allocating medical resources based on cost is to allocate based on something else. First-come,first-served, favoritism and nepotism, arbitrary, or random allocations are all possible. But ultimately someone has to decide who gets which treatment, and who has to go without. This is what Bachmann and Palin meant by death panels: those people who would decide that grandma is too old for a life-saving treatment, even though she can afford it, while little Billy, the Senator's son, has a bright career ahead of him, and should therefore be given preferential treatment. It may sound like fiction, but under a universal healthcare scheme in which prices are not allowed to function, it is the only way to run things.

The death panels happen because someone else is put in charge of making decisions about your life and death, and someone else is put in charge because they are the ones paying the bills, not you. He who pays the piper calls the tune, as the old saying goes. In our admittedly admirable desire to take care of the needy and indigent, we have placed ourselves in a situation where others have the power to dictate our behavior in the name of cost savings in medicine. It is already the case that smoking can get you denied medical treatment. It is not far-fetched to imagine a future in which dietary guidelines are mandatory for those who wish to participate in the health care system, or in which a certain exercise regimen is imposed on the masses from the top down, all in the name of keeping medical costs from rising too high.

On a small scale, we already see this happening. Because doctors hold the exclusive right to prescribe certain medicines, people who want or need those medicines find themselves somewhat at the mercy of their physicians. It is perfectly legal for a doctor to withhold a prescription unless certain conditions are met. He can require that you visit his office a certain number of times per year or that you undergo certain medical tests before refilling a prescription. Nor is this practice limited to addictive and dangerous drugs like opioid-based pain killers; patients have reported losing access to blood pressure medicine and anti-allergy drugs they have taken without incident for years, because their doctor demands frequent office visits.[28] Doctors argue that this practice is for the patients' own good, and that they need to be monitored closely before prescriptions are refilled, but when even routine visits carry a hefty copay, it's hard not to view this practice as a low-level form of extortion.

We are supposed to employ doctors to help us, but we're rapidly entering a reality in which their advice is no longer advice, but a dictate that must be followed, or else.

Against Coercive Medicine

Attempts to modify patient behavior as a requirement for insurance is only one way in which the medical profession exerts control over the population at large. Medicine is also rife with coercion, in which people are administered drugs or surgeries without their consent

---

28 Anne Polta, "When Does a Patient Need to Be Seen?" *Center for Advancing Health*, July 28, 2014.

"for their own good." Dr. Thomas Szasz, a Hungarian psychiatrist and the 20th century's most staunch opponent of coercive medicine, put special stress on the relationship between doctor and patient. A patient, he argued, is a role assumed by someone who voluntarily consents to treatment. A patient wants to be a patient, just as a doctor wants to be a doctor. These words are not objective descriptions of the persons involved, but rather the specific roles they choose to play at a particular moment in time.

Someone who receives medical treatment against his will is not a patient, but rather a victim of assault. Someone who administers treatment against the victim's will is not a doctor, but an attacker. Nevertheless, the medical establishment has tried to alter these descriptions so that a third party — always an expert of some kind — can designate people as patients whether they want to be or not, justified by some alleged deviation from the norm of human anatomy or behavior.

It is true that medical ethics dictates informed consent when it comes to patient care, but it is not uncommon for courts to overrule this very sensible protection of patient rights. We live in an age where the cult of Health, with a capital H, is held to be the highest moral good. People who are not healthy, and especially those who choose not to be healthy, are looked upon with the highest contempt. Fat people, smokers, and drug addicts are among the only people you are still allowed to make fun of. It's hard to find an urban twenty-something who doesn't have a gym membership, engage in CrossFit, Pilates, yoga, or some kind of aerobics, and who doesn't profess to some variety of vegetarianism, veganism, gluten-free, Keto, or paleo diets. What is and is not permissible to eat is a leading topic of conversation at the office and around the water cooler. We are, in a word, obsessed.

Obsession is not always a bad thing, but it usually is. It means that other things — important things — are neglected in service of one overriding preoccupation. Raising health to the highest priority has the unfortunate consequence that people who want to engage in unhealthy behaviors are stigmatized at best, and stripped of their basic human rights at worst.

For example, some religions forbid certain kinds of medical care. Jehovah's Witnesses won't accept blood transfusions. Christian Scientists won't take any medicine at all. We may regard these beliefs as strange or even foolish, but it is not our right to tell others how to live their lives. Still, the courts have decided in certain cases that families raised in these faiths should not be permitted to make their own medical decisions.[29] The child of a Jehovah's Witness who needs a blood transfusion will likely be forced to get one, even if the child himself doesn't want it, because society thinks it knows better than the parents.

There is a legitimate argument to be made about the limits of parental rights, children's ability to consent, and the boundaries of child abuse, and we should have that argument. At what age can a child make her own decisions? Prior to that age, who should make those decisions, the parent or the state? Where is the line between neglect and reasonable difference of opinion? These are difficult questions, to be sure, but it should be troubling at least to everyone that the legal system feels comfortable demanding that some people undergo medical treatments they do not want.

---

29 "Government Pressing Death Cases of Six Children Against Christian Scientists," *Christian Research Institute*, April 13, 2009.

If health is the highest good, then anyone who chooses to be unhealthy must be, on some level, irrational, and irrationality is then used as justification for interfering in a person's choices, on the assumption that they are not qualified to make their own decisions. In reality, people pursue happiness in many diverse ways, not all of which we are going to understand or agree with. It is only proper that we demonstrate humility by accepting that we do not know what is best for all people at all times, and that our idea of the ideal life may differ from that of other people. One may want nothing more than to live to a hundred, and in order to achieve that goal he may run ten miles a day, eat nothing but soy and green vegetables, and refrain from vice of all kinds. Another man might find a hundred years of such living a punishment worse than death, and prefer to sacrifice twenty years of his life in order to be able to have a bag of chips or a glass of whiskey every now and then. Recall what Mises said about rationality: when you call someone irrational, all you are really saying is that you would do things differently in his place. It is a statement of preferences, not of fact, and the laws of subjective value that revolutionized the field of economics do not cease to apply when dealing with health.

Mind Games

Nowhere is the problem of involuntary medicine more acute than in the field of mental health. Ordinarily, it is assumed that consent is required to administer a medical treatment. But the ability to consent originates in the mind. If the mind itself is sick, unable to formulate coherent thoughts and unable to understand what consent means, what is the well-meaning doctor to do? Here again, the power of consent is handed off to a third party, sometimes a family member, sometimes the state. But here is the difficult question in all of this: how do you know when someone is too mentally ill to be able to consent?

First, it should be noted that consent is a legal concept, not a medical one. In America, children under 18 are generally not allowed to consent to things, even when they are perfectly capable of understanding the consequences. Whether or not a mental patient can consent to become a patient in the first place has less to do with his actual mental state, and more to do with the judgment of a court of law. Mental incompetency is typically demonstrated, when it has to be demonstrated at all, through the testimony of so-called experts who decide, without much input from the patient, whether or not he is competent to run his own affairs.

In some cases, this might well be justified. There are objective diagnoses of brain damage and deterioration that can be used to demonstrate that a key part of the brain used for critical thinking is missing or damaged. Victims of head trauma and those suffering from diseases like neurosyphilis or Alzheimer's disease can be definitively shown to have reduced brain function using objective medical tests. But what about the mentally ill, as distinguished from the brain-damaged? How are we to demonstrate, objectively, that they can't be trusted to refuse medical treatment when it suits them?

The field of mental illness is a slippery one, full of euphemisms and misleading vocabulary. When we say someone is "mentally ill" we are alleging that his mind is sick. This is a strange thing to claim, as the mind is not a body part, but rather a name we give to a process which takes place within the brain. The mind is a fairly abstract concept, like the imagination or the emotions. You can't really say that someone has a sick imagination or is emotionally sick, at least not without being metaphorical to the point of obscurity. The people who talk about mental illness tend to claim that it is really a disease of the brain rather than the mind, yet in that case it is unclear why psychiatrists are employed to use talk therapy instead of neurologists and neurosurgeons to fix the affected regions of the brain.

The fact is that most of what is now called mental illness cannot be seen in the brain by any objective methodology. There are no lesions or tumors to mark a gambling addict or a suicidally depressed person. Doctors infer their mental state from their actions and their words, because cutting open their heads and looking inside would reveal a perfectly normal, healthy brain. This is a problem when it comes to demonstrating mental incompetence in a court of law, and so doctors use terms like "chemical imbalance" to account for erratic behavior, even though no such imbalance can be proven, much less demonstrated to deprive someone of rational thought.

The chemical imbalance theory is a convenient one, because it can account for just about anything. There are lots of chemicals in the brain, and they change levels constantly as we go about our daily lives. Our brain chemistry changes when we study a new language, eat food we enjoy, sleep, watch a scary movie, or see a loved one for the first time in a while. All of these situations could be said to cause an imbalance, for the simple reason that there is no *balance* to begin with. An imbalance can only occur in contrast to a balance, but there is no configuration of brain chemicals that could reasonably be called balanced, except perhaps in a corpse, when all brain activity has ceased. In other words, we need to know what constitutes *normal* levels of brain chemicals before we can call a given level *abnormal*, and since these levels are forever changing, normalcy cannot reliably be determined.

In his book *The Emperor's New Drugs*, psychologist Irving Kirsch points out the experimental evidence for the use of antidepressant medications. Such drugs operate on the chemical imbalance theory, but importantly, different drugs assume different types of imbalances. Therefore, one antidepressant operates on the assumption that too much serotonin causes depression, while another assumes that too little serotonin is to blame. Give both these drugs to patients exhibiting the same symptoms, and what happens? If it were true that too much serotonin caused depression, then we would expect the first drug to work, and the second drug to exacerbate the problem. In fact, what we see is similar results for both drugs. Sugar pills — chemically neutral placebos designed to do nothing at all — also provoke a similar response.

In the last chapter, we learned that the scientific method involves coming up with a hypothesis to explain an observed phenomenon, then performing tests to see whether the hypothesis is correct. But if no tests are capable of determining the truth of a hypothesis — if it is *unfalsifiable* — there's no way for science to answer the question of whether it is true or not. The chemical imbalance theory is attractive to many, precisely because it can be maintained in spite of any experimental evidence to the contrary.

Acting Crazy

If neither neuroanatomy nor chemical imbalances can be used to demonstrate mental incompetence, we are left with only one thing: behavior. At this point, there is no medical justification for the alleged inability to consent, but nevertheless doctors, most notably psychiatrists claim to be able to infer from conversations and observation that a person is mentally incompetent. Usually this occurs when behavior differs notably from that which is called normal. But here again we are faced with the problem of what constitutes normal behavior?

Normalcy, at least as it regards human action, is not a medical categorization either, but rather a social one. What is normal and what is crazy differ over the years as societal norms and attitudes change, and across cultures living at the same point in time. In other words, the designation "normal" is a purely subjective one, left up to the opinion of legal and medical experts who have been given power over individuals by the state. A brief glance around the internet reveals that there is virtually no behavior that is not engaged in by large communities of seemingly rational people. It is up to the experts to pass judgment on them on a case-by-case basis, when the law and the Constitution stand in the way of a desired course of treatment or confinement.

A few examples will be instructive here. The Diagnostic and Statistical Manual (DSM) which categorizes officially recognized mental illnesses and is still used by psychiatrists to this day, listed homosexuality as a mental illness until the astonishingly late date of 1987.[30]

Americans who were attracted to those of the same sex were considered sick, not in their right minds and eligible for involuntary treatment in their own best interests, treatments which could consist of things like shock therapy and involuntary drugging (sometimes known among civilized people as poisoning.).

30 Neel Burton, "When Homosexuality Stopped Being a Mental Disorder," *Psychology Today*, September 18, 2015.

In the Soviet Union, opposition to the Communist Party was considered a mental illness, and dissenters were punished in some pretty unpleasant ways. One of America's founders, Benjamin Rush, a signer of the Declaration of Independence and the father of American psychiatry, considered the consumption of alcohol and excessive patriotic zeal to be signs of mental illness. This great humanitarian locked his own son in an asylum for more than 20 years, largely because the lad had difficulty holding down a steady job, and pioneered treatments/torture devices that prevented patients from moving for long periods of time, and dunked them into ice cold water repeatedly for many hours on end.[31]

These are just a handful of examples to make the point. Many of the behaviors we engage in today would have been thought mad by our forefathers, and lots of things they did seem crazy to us now. The DSM, now in its fifth edition, contains nearly 300 recognized mental disorders, many of which would be regarded by most people as falling well within the bounds of normal human behavior. This is an increase from just over 100 such conditions listed in the first edition of the manual, published in 1952. Indeed, one analysis found that half the U.S. population would be considered mentally ill according to the latest guidelines.[32]

Either Americans have developed 200 new mental disorders over the last 60 years, or psychiatrists are getting much more aggressive in applying "disorder" labels to formerly normal behaviors.

We are eager to slap a label on any deviation from the norm, as well as any behavior that causes us irritation or inconvenience. Very

---

31 Thomas Szasz, *The Manufacture of Madness*, Syracuse University Press, 1997.

32 Robin S. Rosenberg, "Abnormal Is the New Normal", *Slate*, April 12, 2013.

young children, forced to stay seated indoors staring at a blackboard for hours on end, sometimes become unruly. Rather than admit that this is exactly what we would expect from a normal child, we give them Ritalin and call their behavior ADHD. Children who struggle with math, once regarded as simply "not good at math", are diagnosed with something called dyscalculia. The Psychopath Checklist, designed to detect those rare individuals who lack the normal range of human emotions including empathy and remorse, contains vague questions that can be interpreted as applying to almost anyone. Are you glib or charming? Do you get bored easily? Are you cunning or manipulative? Are you impulsive or irresponsible? It's safe to say that these traits can be ascribed to most normal people at one time or another.

As journalist Jon Ronson points out in his book *The Psychopath Test*, a prisoner seeking parole is put in a no-win situation by such questions. If he expresses remorse for his crimes, he's cunning and manipulative, trying to fool the parole board, and therefore a psychopath. If he doesn't express remorse, he's lacking in empathy and therefore also a psychopath.

This is not to say that there are no psychopaths or no kids with ADHD, only that the diagnostic criteria for such disorders can easily be stretched to cover perfectly normal, rational behavior, and do not necessarily indicate the presence of mental illness or an inability to reason properly.

It is possible that all the psychiatrists of days gone by simply got things wrong, and we have it all figured out now, thank goodness. It seems more likely that mental illness is a moving target that depends more on cultural norms than on actual science and medicine.

Who's Mad?

Without objective medical or scientific criteria to tell us who is sane and who is not, we rely on the opinions of experts. These are people who have been trained as professional psychiatrists, who work in mental institutions, and who have made a lifetime study of mental illness. Surely their opinion counts for more than that of the average person. Surely it counts more than mine, you are likely thinking as you read this. That would make sense, but then the world so rarely does.

On multiple separate occasions, journalists have decided to test the proposition that experts can tell who is mad and who is not. By lying about symptoms, these enterprising reporters managed to get themselves committed to mental institutions. No one seemed concerned that they might be faking. No one doubted the stories they told about hallucinations and other abnormal symptoms. And without objective tests for these things, can you really blame doctors for taking their word?

In 1887, journalist Nellie Bly, working on a story for the *New York World*, got herself admitted to the Women's Lunatic Asylum in Manhattan. She got in easily enough, fooling doctors with feigned poverty and insanity. Once inside, she ceased all pretense, told the staff who she was and what she was doing, and clarified that she was definitely *not* insane. No one believed her, assuming her story was a fiction concocted by her diseased mind, and it was only with help from outside that she was eventually able to secure release.

In 1972, psychologist David Rosenhan undertook to replicate Bly's experiment, this time using multiple volunteers who agreed to get committed to multiple hospitals. His eight subjects were easily able to get diagnosed with schizophrenia by claiming to hear voices, and were subsequently committed to mental institutions all over the country. The results were the same as Bly's. When the actors admitted they had been lying and that there were no voices, not one of the hospitals realized their mistake or detected the frauds. The actors were eventually released with a diagnosis of "schizophrenia in remission." Rosenhan published these results in the prestigious journal *Science*, but alas, the experiment seems to have made little impact on how asylums are run.[33]

In all of the above cases, the doctors and staff of the mental facilities refused to believe these professions of sanity. They took unprovable accounts of hallucinations on faith, but regarded any subsequent denial or explanation as merely a further symptom of the disease. Then as now, there was no objective criterion for determining a person's sanity or lack thereof.

This is a problem. As noted before, a hypothesis is of little value unless it can be tested and potentially disproven. If every conceivable result of the test results in a confirmation of the hypothesis, then the test is useless. If acting insane is proof of insanity, and acting sane is also proof of insanity, then there is no reliable test for the condition, and we should be very careful about accepting accusations that a person is mentally incompetent. If doctors, trained for their entire careers in the subject, cannot tell the difference between the sane and the insane, it is logical to question whether anyone can, and if no one can, then is it possible that no such difference exists in the first place?

Psychiatrist Thomas Szasz is quick to point out that insanity is a political label rather than a medical one, used to dispose of those

---

Thomas Szasz, Psychiatry: *The Science of Lies*, Syracuse University Press, 2008.

people who are problematic to society. In the 17th century, the term "witch" was used in much the same way. The eccentric, cantankerous, odd, troublesome, unpleasant relatives and neighbors of more easy-going folk were tarred with the label, and then separated from society where their antics would not have to be endured. The same is true with the concept of insanity today. Elderly relations who become a burden on their families are shunted off to asylums on the pretense of losing their faculties. People who would rather bask in the easy euphoria of a narcotic haze than work for a living are sent to rehab facilities because it makes us uncomfortable to have to look at them. Those who prefer a life on the streets to the 21st century rat race are assumed to be mad, and sent to live in small, confined spaces, the very opposite of what they want.

The U.S. Constitution guarantees due process and the right to a trial by jury, but the person who declares he intends to kill himself can be held against his will — kidnapped seems the most accurate word for it — for three days without a whisper of legal process, a time period which can be lengthened if he refuses to renounce his intentions. There are, of course, plenty of rational reasons to commit suicide, but in our legal system, merely declaring the intention is enough to prove to a judge that those who wish to shuffle off the mortal coil are not competent to make their own decisions.

Doctors Without Orders

The upshot of all this is that the label "mental illness" can be applied arbitrarily to just about anyone, with no medical justification, in order to confine them, drug them, or torture them with no recourse for the patient to prove his sanity. All it takes is the testimony of a couple of experts and a judge apathetic enough to go along with the consensus. So much for individualism. So much for uniqueness. So much for freedom.

Madness is a conclusion arrived at by consensus, not by evidence. After all, millions of people go to church every Sunday, talk to a being nobody can see, and consume what they believe to be the body and blood of a man who died two thousand years ago, and no one bats an eyelash. But if one homeless man says he's Napoleon, we think he ought to be locked up for his delusion. If only the Napoleons of the world had millions of followers and their own city-state, they'd probably fare a lot better. But it's tough to be a minority of any kind.

I'm not saying that no one suffers from delusions, hallucinations, depression, mania, or addiction. Of course they do. What I am saying is that we should be very cautious indeed about using the fact that people suffer as a justification for robbing them of their autonomy, not least because almost anything can, and has been, labeled a mental illness as an excuse to persecute the powerless. The evidence is all around us.

Ever enjoy a bowl of Kellogg's Corn Flakes? I bet most of you didn't know that John Harvey Kellogg was an obsessive health nut. On his large estate, dramatized in the film *The Road to Wellville*, he treated alleged lunatics with a daily regimen of what could generously be termed "far too many enemas". He and his brother invented Corn Flakes as an explicit cure for masturbation, which they believed to be a symptom of serious mental illness.[34] It just

34 Matt Soniak, "Corn Flakes Were Part of an Anti-Masturbation Crusade," *Mental Floss*, March 7, 2018.

goes to show how unjust and arbitrary the world is; while some madmen are locked away in a dark room forever, others get to run massive cereal empires that last generations. Think about that the next time you're chowing down on breakfast.

The psychiatrist wants us to believe that his role is to help people, people in anguish, people in misery, people who suffer. There is no denying that such people exist and that, to the extent they seek help, they should receive it. But only by a strange and perverse logic does helping people consist of violently and forcefully oppressing them with straightjackets, both literal and chemical, with barbaric practices such as insulin shock therapy, lobotomy, electroshock treatment, and solitary confinement. It is not helpful to kidnap people and keep them in a padded cell indefinitely, because they refuse to live their lives how certain experts think they ought to. That is not medicine, it is tyranny.

Our Doctors, Our Masters

First, do no harm. Hippocrates, the father of medicine in ancient Greece understood that the rightful role of the physician was to serve and aid his fellow man. Today, three thousand years later, we seem to have forgotten this simple mantra. For all our technological and theoretical advances in the medical arts, doctors, administrators, insurers, psychiatrists, and bureaucrats have somehow convinced themselves that their purpose is not to serve, but to rule, to impose medicine on the population whether they like it or not, and to demand that behavior conform to an unspecified normalcy that can change at any moment to suit the whims of the powers that be.

Psychiatry can be, and has been, used to persecute the innocent in the name of promoting mental health. Government-provided health care decides whether we live or die, while demanding that we live up to certain centrally-approved lifestyles.

I suppose it is inevitable that anyone given the power of life and death would be apt to abuse that power. After all, Lord Acton reminds us that power corrupts, and absolute power corrupts absolutely. Perhaps it is for this reason that the gods in mythology and religion are generally depicted as jealously guarding that knowledge to keep it out of the hands of us lowly humans. And while it is true that individual doctors provide a great service most of the time, there is undeniably something about the profession, as it has become tangled up in red tape over the years, that seems to deny the primacy of the individual, that demands a certain level of obedience.

I began this chapter by referring to a story by Shirley Jackson; I'll end by reminding you of one by Stephen King. The novel *Misery* is about a writer who, injured in a car accident, is taken in by a local woman who happens to be a fan. As she nurses him back to health, we gradually learn that she has no intention of letting him go, or allowing him to ever fully recuperate. She wants to keep him for herself, forcing him to write his stories as she wants to read them. Caregiver becomes jailer. Patient becomes prisoner. The reason that this is one of King's most terrifying books is that it rings true. We all know that when we are sick, we place ourselves in the power of others. We depend on caregivers to be watchful and faithful stewards during our recuperation, and we trust them to relinquish their role once health has returned. We extend this trust, not because it is earned, but because we have no choice. Deep down, I think we all realize that the power to heal goes hand in hand with the power to destroy.

PART FOUR

Government

I've saved the section on government for last because, in a way, it sums up everything that has come before and provides the most complete example of what I have been talking about. Nowhere is the difference between claimed motives and actual outcomes more pronounced, and nowhere is the cognitive dissonance of ordinary people more cumbersome than in the way we talk and think about government.

In the previous sections of the book, I have given examples of the way government controls people. Government schools indoctrinate and imprison, government economists engage in wide-scale behavior modification, government health agencies restrict our access to medicine, and government doctors lock us away for being just a little too different. In this section, I hope to synthesize all these examples into a convincing case that government's claim to work *for* us is the greatest ruse ever perpetrated on the American people.

As ever, we can find clues to how people really think based on the way they express themselves. The language that we use reveals contradictions at work, and the depths of our confusion about this subject. Government employees and elected officials are frequently referred to as "public servants." The president "serves" a term in office. Politicians running for office talk about the need to "give something back" or "serve their country."

It is common to muse about the fact that we pay these people's salaries with our tax dollars, and how they really work for us. In school, we are taught that the American government is a democracy. We, the people, are supposed to be in charge, in contrast to the oppressive monarchy from which we escaped, and the numerous autocratic states around the world.

Yet when you look at the way government officials are treated, surrounded by armed guards, transported in limousines and helicopters, given titles such as Commander-in-Chief and Majority Leader, a life of servility is not the impression one tends to get. We treat our politicians like royalty because, for all practical purposes, they are royalty, imbued with powers and privileges far out of reach of the lowly citizens who voted them into office. Self-governance is part of American mythology, in much the same way as the famous incident of George Washington chopping down a cherry tree. It never happened, and we don't govern ourselves. Not even close.

I want to be clear that I am not picking on America. This section focuses on the United States government because I am an American citizen and have lived my whole life here. I am more familiar with it than with the governments of other countries, and therefore more qualified to write about it. I also love my country, and would not wish to live in any other. But the fact that other governments are worse than that of the United States does not mean I should temper my criticism of the system as a whole. "It could be worse" is not a good reason to refrain from pointing out flaws or trying to make things better. It is that sort of thinking that has led us where we are today, under the thumb of a monolithic state that nevertheless insists on masquerading as the people's servant. It is time for that particular fiction to come to an end, once and for all.

What Is Government?

Most people don't think much about government. When they do, they usually default to basic civics lessons, accepting what they have been told a thousand times without really considering it. Government, we are told, promotes law and order, protects the safety of its citizens, provides a level playing field for commerce, and helps the people that most need it. And while there is a certain truth to all of these claims, they are vast oversimplifications that conceal the true nature of government.

Government can be defined in a lot of different ways, but the best definition I have come across is "a monopoly on the use of legitimate force." In other words, what distinguishes government from other institutions is the ability to use violence or the threat thereof, without legal consequences.

Even if you have a mostly positive view of the government, it's hard not to concede this point. Government actors can put people in jail, extract money from people via taxes, even kill people in extreme situations. Government can wage war. If you or I tried to wage war, or indeed do any of the above things, people would quickly intervene to stop us. No one intervenes when government acts, because most people are convinced that it has the right to do things forbidden to us.

Former Massachusetts Representative Barney Frank once said that government is just the name of those things we do together. It's a lovely sentiment, but about as true as that ridiculous, oft-repeated canard that "we are the government." Unless we all draw paychecks from the taxpayers, no, we're not. We do lots of things together that look nothing like government. We go to church together, hold fundraisers together, start businesses together, play sports together, and have big parties, festivals, and fairs together. Communities are capable of community action, hence the name, without government involvement, and we see it every day. Sometimes this cooperation is frivolous, but sometimes it can have huge effects on relieving suffering and making life better for the community as a whole.

Before he was elected president, Barack Obama called himself a community organizer, so he knows perfectly well that government and community are not synonymous. Nevertheless, during his presidency he appeared to embrace Frank's philosophy, most notably in his famous "You didn't build that" comment, in which he argued that success is not individual, but something to be shared with society as a whole. These sorts of comments seem calculated to persuade people to accept government action under the false premise that it is really just community action, which of course it isn't.

And while communities do lots of things that don't look like government, government does lots of things that bear no resemblance to what a normal community would ever dream of doing. Communities don't wage multi-decade long wars with far away countries for political, rather than defensive, reasons. Communities don't imprison their residents because of things they do in the privacy of their own homes. Communities don't dictate how, when, and under what circumstances residents can ply their trades in order to earn a living for their families. Communities help each other. Government helps itself.

The other common definition we hear, related to but distinct from the first, is that we are the government, and the government is really us. The word "democracy" comes from the Greek, meaning "rule by the people". We are the people, and therefore we must be ruling ourselves. There are a couple of problems with this, the first being that the United States is not a democracy, but rather a republic, in which citizens vote for other people to represent them, not directly for government policy.

The second issue is again this confusion about individual action. In the chapter on economics, I used the term methodological individualism to describe the idea that only individuals act. If someone commits a murder against someone else from the same community, we don't say that the community attacked itself. That would be absurd. We place the blame rightfully on the individual who committed the act. The same goes for government, or at least it should.

People who argue that "we are the government" are saying that we elect ourselves, we tax ourselves, and we imprison ourselves. This is obviously not true. It is more accurate to say that certain members of the society impose taxes and criminal punishments on other members of the society, which is not the same thing as a self-inflicted injury.

The Consent of the Governed

Government derives its authority, and claims its legitimacy from the consent of the governed; at least this is the story we are told by the defenders of the state and all its actions. In an extension of the above, "we are the government" argument, it is often argued that we implicitly consent to everything the government does, merely by continuing to live in the country and voting in elections.

Why is it that consent can only be withdrawn by physically leaving the country? Babies do not ask to be born here; they have no say in the matter, so by what logic does this accident of geography constitute affirmative consent, especially of a child incapable of giving it?

The "implied consent" view is rather a strange one and yet, like most convincing if fallacious arguments, it contains a grain of truth.

On an individual level, it is nonsense to say that we consent to everything government does. If this were the case, you would never see protests, petitions to change laws, civil disobedience, or politicians running on reform platforms. In 2008, Barack Obama won the U.S. presidential election in a landslide by promising "change". If everyone in America tacitly consents to government policy, why was this message so persuasive? The reality is that, while we may agree with some of the things government does, we are not really given any choice to withhold our consent, at least not as individuals.

French political theorist Etienne de la Boetie expressed frustration with the existence of tyrannical governments in Europe, and began to ponder the question of why people allowed tyranny to happen. He argued that it should be impossible for one man, a king or dictator, to rule over a people numbering in the millions without their consent. In most cases, the population could overpower its rulers through sheer force of numbers, or else disobey the law on so massive a scale that the government would be powerless to prevent it. There's some truth to this. If everyone in America stopped paying taxes tomorrow, there's really nothing the government could do to force them. Sure, it could make a few examples out of lawbreakers, but there are not enough jails in the country to hold everyone, not enough courts to process them, probably not even enough members of the military who would be willing to take up arms against more than 300 million conscientious objectors. Even the cruelest, most bloodthirsty dictator could be overwhelmed by his subjects if they resolved to act in a body.

The problem with this line of reasoning is that, of course, people do not act in a body, but as individuals, and for the individual, the price of disobeying or rebelling against government authority is unacceptably high. The fact that most people opt for self-preservation over futile revolt does not constitute consent, any more than a victim of an armed kidnapper refusing to risk escape could be said to consent to being held.

Two Methods of Generating Wealth

My characterizations of government power above may seem overly harsh to many readers. What about all the good government does? What about the national parks and programs to help the poor? What about grants to encourage scientific research, and watchdog agencies who prevent fraud or false advertising? Surely, these are not outweighed by a few corrupt officials or misguided policies, right?

I hope my point of view will seem more reasonable when I explain why the fundamentals of government render it predisposed to oppress and control its citizens. Let's start with an analysis by German sociologist Franz Oppenheimer. In his book, *The State*, Oppenheimer identified two ways to accumulate value (i.e. money): the economic means, and the political means. The economic means of accumulating value simply involves providing a good or service that other people want and are willing to pay for. If you do something well enough, people will buy it, and your fortunes will grow. It is fashionable to call capitalism a philosophy of greed and selfishness, but it's important to remember that the only way to make money in a capitalist system is do things that benefit other people. If you're not helping anyone, no one will pay you, and you will starve. Tough but fair.

Oppenheimer's second method for making money is what he called the political means. This involves taking other people's earnings from them through the use of superior force. When a warlord conquers a village and loots their coffers, he is employing the political means. He has not provided any value, and no money has been given to him voluntarily. He takes what he wants, because he can. That's politics, baby.

The question we have to answer is this: how does our government get its money? You can argue that government does produce value. It provides defense, schools, highways, and a myriad of other services that we could not do without. But remember that value is subjective. Something is only worth what people are willing to pay for it. We don't know how much people would be willing to pay for the things government does, because we are not given a choice. We are forced to pay via our taxes, or else face fines and imprisonment. Even though my sister and I didn't attend school, our parents still had to pay for it. Even though I don't drive a car, I still have to pay for roads, as well as the salaries of traffic cops and meter maids. Without the option of withholding money for things we don't want or need, how do we know whether we are getting a good value for our money or not? We can't.

Maybe you would voluntarily pay more than you currently pay in taxes for the services government provides. A lot of people claim they would. If you feel this way, it is a simple matter to write a check to the U.S. Treasury and contribute what you feel you owe. It may surprise you to learn that few people avail themselves of this option, despite all the rhetoric about social responsibility and paying one's fair share.

We often talk about government funding or the government spending its money on various things, but the truth is that government has no money of its own, because it doesn't produce anything. All the money government has it must first take from the people who earned it, and we call these takings taxation. Anything government does, it *must* do on your dime, and mine, whether we like it or not.

The salient point is the lack of choice. A burglar may rob you, then selflessly spend all the proceeds on starving orphans, but I suspect there would be few who would not still consider this a crime. Good intentions or not, good *results* or not, the lack of choice makes this a perfect fit for Oppenheimer's definition of the political means of wealth accumulation.

Taxation Is Theft

Everyone grumbles about taxes, and rightfully so. We work hard all year round to earn money for ourselves and our families, and then come April 15, a large chunk of what we have managed to scrape together is snatched away by the government. It doesn't seem fair, does it? Barack Obama would be quick to point out no one lives and works in a vacuum, that we all depend on help from our fellow man, and that those who see further have stood on the shoulders of giants. "You didn't build that," he famously said. "Somebody else made that happen."[35] What he neglected to mention was that the "somebody else" to whom we owe part of our success has already been compensated for his own work. The foundations that make modern society possible were not laid out of pure altruism. People "made that happen" because it was in their self-interest to do so. In other words, they got paid. It is double counting to now say that a carpenter should not be allowed to keep his earnings because he didn't first invent the screwdriver or the circular saw.

Benjamin Franklin viewed taxes as an inevitability, famously

35 Eugene Kiely, "'You Didn't Build That' Uncut and Unedited," *FactCheck.org*, July 23, 2012.

using the phrase "death and taxes" to describe the only two things that you can really count on in life. But just because something is ubiquitous doesn't make it right.

Politics depends heavily on euphemism. You'd be amazed at what people can get away with when you can convince them to call things by different names. Ordinarily, when one person takes money from another person without their consent, we call it stealing. But for some reason, when one person is called a tax collector and there are sufficient quantities of paperwork involved, people not only accept it without outrage, but endorse it as a patriotic and civic duty.

People get *angry* when they find out someone else hasn't paid their taxes, even when it is done in a completely legal way through deductions and writeoffs. They argue that we *owe* our taxes to society, and that avoiding that responsibility is cheating everyone else out of their just desserts.

But in what sense are taxes *owed*? It is true that government uses the money to perform services, some of which benefit us. But we didn't ask for these services. Personally, I don't want to pay the FDA to withhold medicine from sick people. I don't want to pay farmers to grow more corn than we need so that they can keep the price down. I don't want to pay soldiers to go fight in Syria and Yemen. I don't want to pay for radio stations I don't listen to or TV stations I don't watch. And even when I do want something, like police protection or the fire department, I never agreed to the terms of the transaction or was given an opportunity to seek out a competitor.

If you come home one day to find your house painted and your lawn mown, without your knowledge or consent, you have no obligation to pay the person who did the painting and the mowing. You may appreciate the work, but you didn't ask for it or agree on a price.

We don't owe our taxes, our taxes are taken from us, under threat of imprisonment. If we behaved the same way towards our neighbors, the charge would be one of unambiguous theft. Why do tax collectors get a free pass?

Financial obligation is a two-way street; it depends on a voluntary agreement between two or more parties. No one else can unilaterally create an obligation against you without your permission.

The Greatest Fallacy

Talking of obligations reminds me of perhaps the most disturbing, yet pervasive, idea I encounter, day after day. The greatest fallacy I see again and again, particularly among young people, but no one is wholly immune, is the notion that, "because I have needs, it is society's obligation to fulfill them." This is the idea that the world owes you something, simply by virtue of you existing. There can hardly be a more dangerous and irresponsible frame of mind, yet I fear it has become the rule rather than the exception among modern Americans.

In the musical *Rent*, it is implied that, because the characters need a place to live, anyone who would fail to provide them with one, or would expect money in return for such a service, is a bad person. Because people need medical care, it seems outrageous that they should have to pay for it. Because money is a necessity of life, everyone is owed a good job and living wage.

Of course, all this is nonsense. We come into the world with nothing, and there's no reason to expect that the others with whom we share our planet, and who have managed to claw back the creeping tendrils of starvation, disease, poverty, and want, have any obligation to make things easier for us. They owe us nothing, but if we want to stay alive, we had better find some way of making ourselves useful to them. If you don't want to live the squalid life of a hunter-gatherer, scrounging out a meager existence in some remote wooded area, you'll need to demonstrate that you can provide a service to others, and hope that they will be willing to share some of their accumulated fortune in return.

It sounds harsh, and of course there is plenty of room for compassion and charity. I think it's a very good thing when people are willing to help others who need it (particularly when it is done out of genuine good feeling and bonhomie rather than the more self-serving purposes outlined in this book.) But just because it's nice to be charitable doesn't mean people *owe* you charity. Once again, you can't impose a financial obligation on someone unilaterally, and against their will. Still, this has not stopped people from believing that a certain amount of wealth is their birthright.

Going back to Oppenheimer, the only alternative to voluntary exchange or total self-sufficiency is to take what doesn't belong to you by pure force. Most people are brought up to believe that stealing is wrong, but if what you are stealing is *owed* to you, well, then it's not really stealing, is it?

This rationale has served warlords and pirates well over the millennia, but not everyone can be a tough, macho gang leader able to take what he wants and get away with it. Some of us are rather quiet, bookish types who would prefer to leave all that dirty business of looting to the professionals, and that's where government comes in.

Unfortunately, a lot of what government does is essentially the outsourcing of the nasty business you and I don't want to do ourselves. If you want a higher wage, you may not be able to persuade your employer to give you a raise, but you can persuade government to raise the minimum wage, and threaten your employer with legal ramifications if he doesn't comply. You may want to build a new library, but lack the resources to build one. No worries, government can collect the money from people who don't care about libraries, but do care about the threat of going to jail if they refuse to pay.

You've no doubt seen mafia movies in which gangsters demand protection money from shop owners operating within their territory. Shops that refuse to pay get vandalized or even destroyed. Government does the same thing, except it calls protection money by different names, such as licensing fees, permitting costs, inspection fees, and of course federal, state, and local taxes. And instead of vandalism, government enforces these payments through the threat of fines, store closures, and jail time.

All those nice things I mentioned government doing earlier — funding schools, and science, and help for the poor — those are all done by force, using someone else's money, on behalf of people unwilling or unable to coerce their fellow citizens into doing what they want. This does not mean that the poor shouldn't be fed or that children shouldn't be educated — they should — but how can such things claim any moral superiority when they are done at the point of a gun? How can we justify systematically forcing people to do what we want them to do, recognizing that we ourselves lack the courage of our convictions to do it in person?

Magician and libertarian Penn Jillette, in an interview with Bill Maher, once remarked that he would not want government to do anything he himself wouldn't be willing to do. He said that he would be willing to use force to stop a murderer or a rapist, but not to build a library.[36] It sounds silly when said in those terms, but what happens if you refuse to pay the taxes that go towards building libraries? Men with guns come and make you. I don't care how much you like libraries; would you treat your neighbor that way? I wouldn't.

The Myth of the Social Contract

But what about the social contract? Philosopher Jean-Jacques Rousseau argued that the people living within a society have implicitly agreed to treat each other in a certain way, that they are bound by an invisible contract, as it were, to support each other and for each to pay his fair share into the community. Governments are simply ways of enforcing the social contract by holding potential violators to account.

Social contract theory is popular because it is a convenient way of justifying any coercive action on the grounds of contract enforcement. And the reason it can provide such easy justifications is that the contract in question doesn't actually exist. It has no clauses, no disclaimers, no loopholes and, most importantly of all, no signatures. No one can argue that he is complying with the contract, because no one can say for sure what the contract requires. It is an infinitely plastic document that can be stretched to prescribe any behavior we want it to.

No one has seen the social contract, no one can read or consulted it, and no one has agreed to it. I don't remember being asked if I would like to enter into an agreement in which the government can force me to behave in certain ways, take my money, and forbid me from a wide variety of harmless activities in exchange for roads,

36 *Real Time With Bill Maher*, October 14, 2011.

a police force, and a fire department. Given such an offer, it might be reasonable to accept it, but the point is that the offer was never extended in the first place. It was instead imposed on us from on high and then given a *post hoc* justification that, of course, we really *did* agree to it just by existing.

You can't bind people with contracts they never agreed to, or to which they were given no opportunity to opt out. That's not how contracts, social or otherwise, work, but that's not the only problem with the theory. If it were indeed true that Jones is bound by the social contract to pay for Smith's schooling, Smith would be within his rights to take the money from Jones himself, by force if necessary. But of course, such actions are not only impermissible by law, but heavily frowned on by polite society at large. The government is permitted — nay, encouraged — to do things that, if you or I did them, would result in a very long prison sentence indeed. This is yet another clue that there's something rotten in the state of Washington, D.C. Our so-called public servants are allowed to do things that are forbidden to us, and in fact are empowered to directly punish us for coloring outside the lines. In what other servant-master relationship is the servant the one with all the freedom, and all the license to dispense discipline on the masters? Obviously, the question is rhetorical.

Justice Is Blind, Deaf, Walks with a Limp, and Has a Speech Impediment

Almost everyone agrees that, to the extent that government should do anything, its chief responsibility is to protect the lives and property of its citizens from undue aggression.

This is the rationale behind the justice system, and in theory, it's a pretty good idea. Most of us are weak, frail creatures incapable of protecting ourselves from bands of roving marauders, thieves, bullies, axe murderers, and spiteful neighbors, so we outsource the job to an organization with the resources to maintain order, punish transgressors, and compensate victims. Fair enough.

In practice, however, the justice system doesn't quite live up to its admittedly noble ideals. While the idea is to protect the innocent from those that would harm them, it is frequently the case that perfectly harmless people minding their own business suffer severe, sometimes life-ruining victimization at the hands of police and the courts. Sometimes this occurs through error, but just as often it is by design. The reason is much the same as for the other abuses of power I've already outlined. The justice system is more or less unilateral. We have to submit to it, and really have no recourse if things should go badly for us. Individual decisions can be appealed to a higher court, it's true, but you can't appeal against the law itself. The law is the final authority.

In any situation where one institution is given virtually limitless power over people who have no means of fighting back, abuse is bound to occur. Power corrupts, absolute power corrupts absolutely. And while not every person in a position of authority is corrupt — many of them are quite pleasant and moral people — the nature of these institutions enables bad outcomes for the little guy.

This is the reason so many people have such negative opinions of police. You don't have to look very far to see people hurling epithets like "pig" at uniformed officers of the law, verbally abusing them, running from them, and sometimes even assaulting them. The Black Lives Matter movement has basically condemned the entire law enforcement apparatus as racist bullies who get their jollies by shooting unarmed black people just because they can.

Naturally, this position upsets a lot of people. Those who value law and order worry about a war on cops, and see police detractors as little more than hooligans apologizing for criminals. Blue Lives Matter is the title given the counterrevolution in support of police.

As is often the case in mass movements, the two sides are really talking past one another. It is obviously the case that many individual police officers are good people working a difficult job, putting their lives in danger to protect and serve others. They don't deserve to be harassed and bullied for trying to stop criminals from hurting the innocent. On the other hand, it's easy to understand the frustrations of Black Lives Matter if you actually listen to them. There is an undeniable power differential between the police and the average citizen, particularly if that citizen lives in a low income, inner city neighborhood. In the climate of fear and paranoia that results from working a dangerous beat in high-crime areas, police are not immune from stepping over the line, applying too much force, or ignoring basic civil liberties protections. When this happens, the victims see a media ready to take the side of police without question, assuming that the victim must be trash simply because of what he looks like and where he lives. It's rare to see an officer be prosecuted for a crime, at least in a high profile way, and so minorities come to feel that the deck is stacked against them, not without some justification.

Take the case of Eric Garner, the New York City man who was killed by a chokehold applied by an overly zealous police officer. Garner's crime was selling loose cigarettes on the street. He wasn't a rapist, murderer, arsonist, or thief. He was just selling a product to willing customers, without collecting the taxes the New York City government demands in tribute. It's hard to imagine a more minor infraction of the law, but police on the scene acted aggressively in such a way that resulted in Garner's death.[37] In all likelihood, the killing was accidental. I don't think the officer in question intended to choke a man to death, and an underlying health issue may have contributed to Garner's demise. Nevertheless, police are taught that ordinary people have to submit to their authority, and in such an environment, it's all too easy to lose perspective and embrace the idea that might makes right. It would be surprising if such attitudes did not result in needless casualties.

Imagine for a minute what you would do if, all of a sudden, everyone around you was forced to obey your every command without question, or else face severe consequences. How do you think it would affect your psyche or your sense of self-importance? It's easy to claim that we would not abuse the power or take advantage of people, and most people probably wouldn't — at first. But after several months or several years, wouldn't you start to lose your connection to your friends and neighbors? Wouldn't you start to regard them as inferiors? After all, they have to bow to your will. Why would that be the case unless you were somehow better than them? You might start to regard any defiance of your authority as impudent, presumptuous, or just plain wrong. You might start to relish the punishments of those who refused to follow your orders. This is essentially the position police officers are put in, with the added bonus that some of these people are actually trying to kill them. We're practically asking these poor men and women to

37 Al Baker, J. David Goodman & Benjamin Mueller, "Beyond the Chokehold: The Path to Eric Garner's Death," *New York Times*, June 13, 2015.

develop paranoid god complexes. And then we act surprised when innocent people get hurt.

Garner's case is a prominent one, but it is by no means isolated. No-knock raids, in which police are empowered to enter a residence without the owner's permission, have resulted in deaths when police mistakenly entered the wrong house. It is common for family dogs to be shot on sight by police, even when the homeowner has done nothing illegal, and in one case a mistaken entry led to the shooting of a seven-year-old girl, asleep in her bed. In this last case, the officer responsible faced no consequences for his actions.[38]

Then, there's the practice of civil asset forfeiture, a legal loophole that allows police to seize private property without any form of due process, as long as they can claim they suspect the victim of being involved in criminal activity. Innocent people have lost homes, cars, and their life savings due to police wrongly suspecting them of crimes they didn't commit, and even the innocent struggle to regain their property. This is not helped by the incentives in place for police, in which the law allows local departments to keep the proceeds of what they seize, applying the money towards their budgets, and even towards perks like margarita machines for the office.[39]

Civil asset forfeiture is plainly no more than legalized theft, and many states are now working to reform the practice, but there remains much work to be done. Many in the law enforcement community are lobbying against reforms, because they claim they need the money for their operating budgets, disregarding such technicalities

---

38 Kate Abbey-Lambertz, "Charges Dismissed Against Joseph Weekly, Cop Who Shot Sleeping Seven-Year-Old," *Huffington Post*, January 30, 2015.

39 Nick Sibilla, "Cops in Texas Seize Millions by 'Policing for Profit,'" *Forbes*, June 5, 2014.

as the Fourth Amendment, which forbids unreasonable search and seizure, and the Fifth Amendment, which guarantees citizens the right to due process. This is disappointing, but not surprising. Give anyone a license to steal for their own benefit, and don't be shocked when they use it.

The mistake groups on the political left often make is to condemn police officers as people, asserting that they are racist bullies who will take any chance to prove it. Apart from being a sweeping generalization of the kind that anti-racists should abhor on principle, it's simply not accurate. There are undoubtedly bad apples among the police force, as with any large population, but focusing on the individuals misses the broader point. I believe that most police officers are good people, or at least start out that way, forced to operate within a system that incentivizes bad behavior.

If you give people weapons the general public isn't allowed to have, train them to think of all citizens as potential threats, allow them to take money and property for their own benefit at will, and introduce quota systems, like the one for traffic tickets, that encourages arbitrary rather than necessary law enforcement, bad things are obviously going to happen.

The Law Is Not Just Sure, It's Positive

Another part of the problem is the idea, encouraged not only by police academies, but in our public schools as well, that the law is absolute and without error. We're trained to think that legal things are good, and anything that is illegal must therefore also be immoral. This is the philosophy known as legal positivism.

In reality, the law has very little to do with the admittedly complex notions of right and wrong, ethics, or morality. The law doesn't come from some divine ruler on high; it comes from men, ordinary, fallible, mostly not even very bright men. Remember, there's no intelligence test required to get elected to Congress. You don't have to pay attention to politics for very long to realize that no small number of elected representatives probably shouldn't be trusted with sharp objects, much less the laws of the land. The laws they pass are the result of a combination of self-interested calculation, logrolling, compromise, special interest pleading, corruption, and populist pandering. There's no reason to expect the laws that do pass to be good ones, or even to make sense.

Of course, there are good laws. You shouldn't kill, or steal, or rape, or vandalize other people's property. But just because a few laws are consistent with morality, that doesn't mean they all are. There's no obvious connection between morality and a 55-mile per hour speed limit, laws that prohibit certain types of drug use or gambling, occupational licenses, laws that stop you from defending yourself against an attacker in public, or the regulations on what kind of food you're allowed to produce and sell. These laws are more or less arbitrary, and chiefly exist either to protect powerful businesses from competition, to raise money for the government, or just to exercise control over people for the pure sake of it.

Those who know history should be especially sensitive to the arbitrary nature of the law. Remember, until the 1860s, it was legal to own slaves. Alcohol use was illegal during the 1920s. Gay marriage is only recently legal (although some states still have anti-sodomy laws on the books). When laws change so frequently and so drastically, how can anyone hold that we have a moral duty to obey them? Nevertheless, when abuses of the justice system come to light, there is always a crowd ready to grumble, "Well, he should have done as he was told."

Obedience to arbitrary laws may be prudent if we want to stay out of trouble, but it is certainly no moral imperative. In fact, when laws are manifestly unjust, it is usually more moral to disobey them.

Intuitively, we must know this. We celebrate historical rule-breakers like Rosa Parks, who refused to submit to segregationist policies, for the simple reason that such policies were morally wrong. Civil disobedience is an important part of the American tradition, and more important than that, it's often the only way to get things done. Congress has no reason to change or repeal a law that everyone is complying with. It takes a refusal to comply to effect actual change.

As a product of one of the earliest waves of homeschooling in America, I'm particularly sensitive to this reality. You may not realize it, but the fight to legalize educating children at home was not a painless one. The law said that children had to attend schools and that was that. It was only when mothers started disobeying, keeping their children out of school to teach them at home, that the government was faced with a public relations dilemma.

It doesn't look good to be filling jails with mothers whose only crime is to want to teach their own children, but the law was the law. The only way to avoid looking like heartless tyrants was to change it, and so it was changed. If all mothers had agreed to comply with the law, while politely asking for a different policy, there would have been no impetus to action, and homeschooling would likely still be illegal today.

A similar thing happened with medical marijuana laws. Patients with chronic pain, cancer, and other major illnesses started taking cannabis as a legitimate medical treatment, even though they risked imprisonment for it. Putting cancer patients in prison looks pretty bad, and so most states have at least partially legalized the drug, although a few holdouts remain. Without people willing to violate the law, there would have been no reason for governments to take the legalization movement seriously. Disobedience breeds change, yet from the perspective of the justice system, all lawbreakers must be punished. The result is the persecution of good people who are not hurting anyone.

A particularly thorny issue for law enforcement is the idea of the victimless crime. Many people, myself included, regard this as a contradiction in terms. In order for a crime to occur, there must be a victim. If there is no victim, then how can there have been a crime? The point is obvious when you consider what philosophers like to call the Robinson Crusoe scenario. If a man is alone on a desert island, with no one else about, no society, no courts, no nations, and for the sake of argument let's say no animals, what could he do that would be considered a crime? It seems an odd question to even ask. Such a person could not be a criminal, because the very notion of criminality depends on there being someone who is wronged, whose rights are violated, who is made to suffer in some way. No victim, no crime. Sounds simple enough.

Of course, in actual courts of law, this is not the way things are done at all. There are countless instances in which people are held to criminal account for actions which create no identifiable victims at all, the most obvious being the consumption of illegal substances. This does not just include illegal street drugs like cocaine or heroin, but legitimate pharmaceuticals obtained without a prescription, and certain foods not approved by the FDA or else imported from other countries without the proper paperwork, labels, or other regulatory requirements fulfilled. There are quite a few people who wish to consume unpasteurized milk because they believe it to be more healthful than the kind purchased in supermarkets, but in most states, they are forbidden from doing so. If consumption itself is not criminalized, buying or selling the milk is, which, unless you happen to be a dairy farmer, amounts to the same thing.

Drinking milk or taking drugs in the privacy of your own home creates no victim; it is the act of an individual exercising his rights over his own body. Yet, the state can send you to jail for this alleged wickedness if it chooses to. Why? In what sense is this justice? What wrong is being righted by imprisoning people for their — admittedly, sometimes poor — choices? And from where does the state derive the authority to pass such judgment on people's private behavior?

The legal system avoids the victimless crime issue, rather than confronting it, by conjuring up an imaginary victim when otherwise none would exist. We are therefore confronted with the Orwellian phrase "crimes against society," as an obfuscating term designed to help put in chains those who have done no harm to anyone else. If I can refer you back to the section of this book on economics, you will recall that the word "society" is a weaselly sort of word, often used to confuse rather than clarify. Society is not an entity. It does not bleed, it cannot feel pain, it cannot suffer, it has no property and no rights thereto, it can't think, and it certainly can't file a legal claim against an assailant. Society is no more than a group of individuals, and if there are no individuals harmed by an action, it is gibberish to say that society is harmed by it in lieu of real people. Either an action harms some individuals or it does not. If it does, identify the victims and proceed as usual. Otherwise, there is no criminality, and no further action to be taken — at least as far as the law is concerned. All this talk of society merely clouds otherwise clear thinking and results in punishment for the innocent.

Consumption behaviors are far from the only ones that are banned in spite of a lack of victim. Prohibitions on gambling, as well as the almost numberless rules against engaging in commerce with a willing partner without first greasing the palms of various regulatory bodies, consume a staggering amount of legal ink and judicial resources. Even speeding tickets, in most instances, are more a case of extortion than of protecting potential victims. Let the reader ask himself how many times he's been pulled over because he was endangering other motorists, and how many of those times were because he exceeded an arbitrary speed limit while driving perfectly responsibly, and I think the point will be clear. Add to this the fact that many police departments require that a certain number of tickets be issued each month regardless of the number of actual lawbreakers, and you'll see that revenue, not safety, is the overarching goal of such policies.

Do You Really Want to Hurt Me?

I can already anticipate some of the objections to the above. The solitary drug user or gambler, it is often claimed, does create victims. His family, his friends, and anyone else who cares about him may all be made to suffer as a result of his actions. Is it not, therefore, just to stop him before he breaks the hearts of his loved ones?

This is a common objection, and one that rests on a fundamental misunderstanding of the nature of victimhood. It is, of course, true that those who care about a reckless vagabond will be brought to grief through his lack of regard for his own well-being. It is in the very nature of caring about another human being that one is apt to suffer disappointment at their actions, and that disappointment can be very painful indeed. But it is absurd to suggest that, with a view of preventing such disappointments from taking place, the famously impersonal justice system ought to step in and intervene. Once that road is taken, there's nothing to stop the abolition of all free choice whatsoever. This becomes obvious when you realize that the things people value differ from person to person. Something you may regard as a terrible tragedy, I may think a rather good idea. For example, there are traditional families whose members would suffer great anguish if their children got married to someone of another race or religion. There are fathers who are driven to great despair in the knowledge that their sons will not carry on the family business. There are mothers who would rather their children be drug addicts than homosexuals. There are parents who would rather their children were ruined by gambling than move to another country, or get a tattoo, or enlist in the military.

The fact that these decisions can and do bring about tremendous amounts of trauma, grief, and suffering to others does not mean that the government has the right to prevent people from having tattoos, interracial marriages, new careers, new places of residence, or a partner of the same sex. Anyone who suggested that the justice system should do any of those things would be rightly denounced as a fascist authoritarian. But, because we have been brought up to trust the law and the people charged with executing it, most of us have a blind spot for those practices which are already illegal, and have been since before we were born. These things, we reason, *should* be illegal because they *are* illegal, and that's as far as the train of thought goes. It's the same train of thought that allowed people to be content with Jim Crow laws mandating segregation and systematic racism. It wasn't that everyone living in that time period was an incurable racist; it was simply that they were taught to trust the authority of government to the extent that they never thought to question injustices happening right under their noses.

The Ultimate Price

I was introduced to the political philosophy of libertarianism when I was in college. As a more or less random elective, I had registered for a course called "Philosophy and Values" taught by a professor named Tim Hall, whose claim to fame was having been a contestant on the now mostly-forgotten game show *Win Ben Stein's Money*. The class largely consisted of discussions of ethical dilemmas, which I found fascinating, and as I found myself in consistent agreement with Professor Hall, I was interested to learn that he was a libertarian, and that maybe I was too.

I learned a lot in that class, as well as from Professor Hall's seminar explicitly dealing with libertarian theory a year later, but one of the points he made early on in that first class has stuck with me ever since. He pointed out that policymakers should never make laws that they are not prepared to enforce by any means necessary, up to and including lethal force.

At first, this seems like a strange thing to say. The death penalty is becoming increasingly unfashionable, and even where it is still in use, it is only reserved for the most heinous of criminals. Perhaps we should be prepared to kill to stop rapists and murderers, but it's absurd to suggest that that level of threat is necessary to stop jaywalkers and loiterers, isn't it?

Actually, all law enforcement rests implicitly on the threat of deadly force. It has to, or else it doesn't work. To see why, let's follow the case of a hypothetical conscientious objector. Suppose you get a parking ticket and, feeling that the fine is unjust and unfair, you refuse to pay it. What happens? You'll get fined for failure to pay, and then another fine, and then maybe another. But since the initial ticket was unjust, by extension all of these fines are as well, and you continue in your refusal to pay. Next, you might get a subpoena to appear before a court, or you might have your driver's license suspended. Ignore these demands, as you have ignored the previous ones, and a warrant will be put out for your arrest. Now, you've got men with guns chasing you, perhaps trying to take away your freedom, all over a parking ticket! If you resist the arresting officers, as your principles require you to, and if you are forceful and effective enough in so doing, sooner or later, you're going to get shot, maybe even killed, because you didn't think it was right to pay a parking ticket. Think it can't happen? Think this is hyperbole? Remember Eric Garner.

The above paragraph is not really a criticism of the justice system. It has to be that way. If the state showed leniency on people who refused to acknowledge subpoenas or drove around with suspended licenses, soon everyone would be doing it, and there would be no reason to obey the law at all. As long as one side escalates, the other side has to escalate as well, or else the system breaks down completely. Nevertheless, it's important that we understand that this is how law enforcement works. Since laws can only be enforced effectively with the threat of deadly force, we should ask ourselves whether all of the laws passed by Congress and state legislatures are important enough to kill for.

Next time you get a haircut, muse about whether an unlicensed barber is a criminal worthy of this threat. Next time you drive past a farm, ruminate on whether people should be threatened for refusing to pay corn subsidies, or whether the farmer himself should be harassed if he chooses to sell milk or eggs without the FDA's approval. Next time you go into a library, look around and wonder, "Is this really worth all the intimidation and implied violence that had to go into making it?"

Every time the government undertakes a project with taxpayer money, the implication is clear: "you are paying for this, even if we have to kill you to make you." I think if more people understood this principle, there would be a lot less complacency over the reams and reams of new legislation casually passed by our elected officials each and every year.

Jailhouse Rock

Obviously, most people don't die as a result of breaking the law. Few indeed are the civil disobedients principled and crazy enough to allow things to get that far. Mostly, lawbreakers just end up in prison. Then, after a specified period of time, they are let out of prison again. What's really strange is the number of people who seem to think that this system makes any sense whatsoever.

Think about it: commit a crime, get locked away from society for years, while any skills, education, or relations you might have had start to decay, and then get released back into the wild with a big stamp on your forehead that says "Don't hire me." This is the system, mind you, that we are assured is supposed to reduce crime and keep us more safe. One could hardly come up with a more ridiculously ineffective idea if one tried. A line from the film adaptation of *A Clockwork Orange* always comes to mind when discussing the issue of prisons. "Cram criminals together and see what happens. You get concentrated criminality, crime in the midst of punishment." The sharp social commentary of Anthony Burgess could hardly be more apt.

It may make sense to separate violent killers from a society of potential victims, but for those who are expected to be released and try to go on with their lives, how does prison help either the victims, the criminals, or anyone else in the community? In the case of a robbery, for example, the law does not require that the victim be made whole. The only compensation for the theft is the knowledge that the robber is being punished. The robber himself, who may well have been motivated more by financial desperation than by pure malice, is sent to dwell in the company of hardened criminals for a few years, where he will be mentally and physically abused before being released on parole with virtually no chance of finding a decent job. We then expect him not to fall back on his old ways, nor resort to using any of the criminal tips and tricks he doubtless picked up on the inside, which seems naive at the very best. Finally, the other members of the community — who have done nothing wrong — are forced to pay for the criminal's trial, food, housing, and clothes, and medical care for the duration of his prison stint through their taxes, and content with the knowledge that they have just as much chance as anyone of being the criminal's next victim when he once again finds himself unemployed and desperate. It is a system in which no one is helped, and everyone is hurt.

Whenever you see a deliberately designed system that apparently benefits no one, you have to either assume sheer incompetence or that there's more going on than meets the eye. We are told that the goal of the prison system is to reduce crime, but upon examination, it practically incentivizes it by creating a class of ex-cons steeped in criminal culture and generally unable to find honest work upon release. Maybe the people who designed and maintain the system are really bad at their jobs, which would not surprise me. Or maybe the stated goal and the real goal of the system are two entirely separate things, which would surprise me even less.

If the purpose of prison is not to keep us, the citizenry, safe, then what is the purpose? It is clearly not to mete out justice, because justice would involve restitution for the victims, some kind of compensation for the loss they have suffered via a debt worked off over time by the offender. That doesn't happen. The goal is not to make criminals better people through rehabilitation, since prison has the exact opposite effect, making prisoners more violent, damaged, and reviled by their community. Given all these factors, it seems to me that the true purpose of prisons can be one of two things — most likely a combination of both: first, to provide a favor to the people who build, own, and operate prisons by guaranteeing a consistent source of revenue and cheap labor, and second, to keep the general population in line, obedient, docile, and just fearful enough of their government that they toe the line. In other words, prisons are used to punish rule breakers and troublemakers, not provide justice or safety for the innocent. And punishment, without a secondary, more noble goal, is pure cruelty and domination.

These kinds of bait-and-switch policies in which we are told one thing in order to conceal what is really going on are common in government. When Donald Trump became president, pro-immigration activists became furious at his proposal to build a wall on the

Mexican-American border. He was called a racist, insensitive to the plight of poor people from Latin America looking for opportunity and prosperity in America. These are legitimate complaints, but it was remarkable how few people, most prominently among them the libertarian firebrand Ron Paul, pointed out that a wall can just as easily be used to keep people in as it can to keep people out.

War Is the Health of the State

I've talked a lot about the justice system and the state's monopoly on the use of force. The logical extension of that is the military's adventures overseas. If law enforcement uses the threat of violence to keep Americans in line at home, the military flexes its muscles to control the people and governments of other countries.

War used to be a life or death struggle to achieve specific ends. Countries went to war to drive back marauding hordes of would-be conquerors, to gain independence or freedom from tyranny, as well as for several less noble, yet still concrete, reasons. Today, war has become a sort of default posture with many nations, without any achievable, or even identifiable, objectives. When there is no goal to be accomplished, there is no reason to end the wars and bring the troops home. One can hardly declare "Mission Accomplished" when the mission doesn't depend on actual accomplishments.

The Constitution states that Congress has the sole responsibility for declaring war, but it has not actually done so for many decades. So, how are all these wars going on without congressional approval? The answer is that most members of Congress don't want the responsibility for sending American soldiers to their deaths — it's not great PR for the next election — so they have abdicated their duty to the president and his generals. Today, wars are no longer declared. Instead, we are involved in "military conflicts," which are distinguished from wars only in that they earn a higher score in Scrabble.

The problem is so bad that it's actually impossible for anyone to say how many wars the United States is currently waging. Seven is a popular number, but depending on who you ask and how you define a war, the estimate can range from zero to over 40. It's hard for the voters to hold politicians accountable for excessive warmongering when they can't even find out how many wars are going on, or where, or why.

This lack of accountability is coupled with the relentless and deliberate nurturing of fear in the American public. From the stories we see every day on the 24-hour news networks, to the messaging coming out of the White House and the Pentagon, we're told over and over again that the world has never been more dangerous, and that only through continued war efforts in faraway countries can we have any hope of survival.

It's not true, of course. As Harvard sociologist Steven Pinker points out in his twin treatises, *The Better Angels of Our Nature* and *Enlightenment Now*, it's actually far more accurate to say that the world has never been safer. You just don't hear about it because that narrative doesn't sell newspapers or F-15s.

While it's true that there are now fewer casualties resulting from war than in most times in human history, the amount of money and resources — many of which are human — involved in the war machine is simply staggering. For example, the war in Afghanistan has now been going on for so long that the youngest soldiers eligible for combat were not even born when the war started. After

18 years and an obscene amount of money spent, what have we actually accomplished there, and can anyone honestly say that we are better off for it? Nor is there any end in sight. If our attitude towards military intervention continues unchanged, we could easily spend another 18 years there. Sen. John McCain, who never saw a war he didn't like, made an uncharacteristically candid comment when he said that he was prepared for our troops to spend 100 years in the Middle East if necessary.[40] Of course, most people's definition of "necessary" will probably differ considerably from McCain's.

The irony is that all these wars that are justified using our fear of terrorism or foreign aggression actually make us *less* safe. The consequence of keeping soldiers out in the field, engaged in dangerous and exhausting work, for multiple tours of duty is that people burn out. The ceaseless nature of overseas combat means that talented soldiers, instead of waiting for when they are needed, get chewed up and spit out by the machine, never seeing their families, mentally and emotionally exhausted. Should there ever come a time when we need a robust force of elite soldiers to defend our shores, we will regret having squandered that talent and energy on such trivial exercises overseas.

We call military employment "service" and say that soldiers are going to "serve" their country. In the case of most enlisted personnel, I don't really dispute this classification for once. A pilot or medic or marine shipped off to Yemen or Syria or Afghanistan usually has no designs on controlling innocent people, but instead simply wants to stop bad actors from causing harm in the world. Here, the soldiers themselves are victims of the help-as-control confusion, having

40 "McCain defends '100 Years in Iraq' Comment," *CNN*, February 15, 2008.

been told by their superiors that they are making the world safe for democracy, when in fact they are expected to sacrifice their lives, their health, and their sanity while being pawns in a geopolitical game that actually has nothing to do with protecting the homeland.

The military-industrial complex, like all unaccountable government agencies, exists to perpetuate itself and to enrich those who run it. If you're an arms manufacturer, a military contractor, or a high-level general resting comfortably within the safety of the Pentagon, war is simply good for business.

The Death of Federalism

When we talk about the government, we tend to think of the politicians and bureaucrats in Washington, the president, the White House, Congress, the Supreme Court, and numberless regulatory agencies from the IRS to the EPA. This is understandable, as these are by far the most visible and intrusive forms of government that not only consume the most resources, but gobble up the lion's share of media coverage.

This was not the way it was meant to be. The Constitution was specifically designed to preserve the autonomy of state and local governments, with the federal government merely serving as a common framework to promote commerce and protect individual rights. The Tenth Amendment, the last in the Bill of Rights, affirms that any power not specifically granted to the federal government — and there's only a handful in the Constitution — shall be reserved to the states or to the people. This means that, in theory anyway, it's actually illegal for the federal government to tell the states what to do with their laws, except in certain narrowly-defined situations.

In practice, it hasn't worked out that way. Through a combination of the courts' creative interpretation of the straightforward text of the Constitution, and the abuse of a number of loopholes and workarounds, states find themselves almost completely subservient to Washington, rather than the other way around.

One of the most effective tools the feds have for exerting control over the states is funding. Money may not buy happiness, but it can certainly buy obedience. Here's how it works: the federal government levies taxes against the citizens of the several states, then offers to give some of that money back, but only if state governments abide by certain conditions or take certain actions. It's bribery, but with the cruel twist that people are being bribed with their own money.

In the Education chapter, I talked about the Race to the Top and Common Core programs, programs designed to standardize education practices across the states. Defenders of Common Core were fond of arguing that the program was not a federal mandate, and that it was implemented voluntarily by governors. These claims are, in the strictest technical sense, true, but they are also wildly misleading. The truth is that states were offered large amounts of money to implement the standards. And while they technically could have declined, what governor wants to be on the receiving end of charges from his political opponents that he turned down millions of dollars in education funding? In short, it was an offer they couldn't refuse.

Education is only one prominent example, with transportation funding and Medicare constituting major levers the federal government can use to extract compliance from the states. The carrot-and-stick method of either withholding funding or promising additional grants is a common way for the federal government to exceed its constitutional authority and demand fealty from the smaller, localized governments across the country.

What Measure a Politician?

Like lawyers, politicians are an object of popular ridicule. In works of satire, they are consistently portrayed as corrupt, incompetent, and dishonest, eager to fleece the voters for personal gain. It is not the type of stereotype you would expect to see for someone who is truly a servant of the public. Indeed, we seldom ridicule those who work on our behalf or who devote themselves to making our lives better. Satire has always been a tool for the oppressed to mock the oppressor. Comedy is a tool by which the weak can get the upper hand over the strong.

The reason the very First Amendment to our Constitution protects freedom of speech and of the press is to make sure that the lowly citizens would be free to criticize people in power, calling them out for their bad behavior, and mocking them when such mockery was deserved (which it almost always is). The Founders did not want to create a country, like so many in the Europe they had fled, that would stifle any criticism under the threat of violent reprisal. They recognized how important it was to limit the power of politicians.

Even this straightforward, extremely sensible precaution, was of limited effectiveness, however. Our second president, John Adams, signed the Alien and Sedition Acts into law, allowing him to persecute Americans who dared criticize his decisions as president, or make fun of him via humorous newspaper cartoons. Abraham Lincoln, whom everyone remembers as being a champion of freedom, made it illegal to criticize the Civil War or its goals. Our current president, the notoriously thin-skinned Donald Trump, has wished aloud on more than one occasion that he could "open up" libel laws to prosecute his detractors.

Servants don't threaten their masters when their performance is critiqued, but it is not uncommon at all for the master to become cross and punish his servants over a harmless joke or snide remark. The political class, not content with all the power they already have in being able to make laws, live off the taxpayer dime, command television appearances whenever they like, and secure lucrative consulting or publishing contracts seemingly at will, want to deny the people who elected them and who pay their salaries even the dignity of humor or complaint.

This leads us to an obvious question: what sort of person would want such a job, and what sort of person is likely to get it? When you think about it, an election is basically an extended job interview. The candidate tries to convince his voters that he or she will be the best person for the job over weeks and months of campaigning, and ultimately the voters decide whether to believe it or not. At first glance, it seems like a pretty good system, but like actual job interviews, it has its drawbacks.

In *The Case Against Education*, Bryan Caplan devotes a great deal of space to the ways in which employers make hiring decisions. They rely upon college degrees, even when those degrees have little to do with the actual work required, because the ability to acquire a degree signals certain qualities the employer desires. For example, anyone able to complete four years of college must be dedicated, patient, able to follow rules, and more or less a conformist.

Companies like dedicated conformists, because they are easy to manage. They may not be brilliant, they may not be original, but at least they can get to work on time and do as they're told. This is why so many wildly intelligent and creative dropouts struggle to find success in the working world. A college degree says little about their abilities, but it says a lot about their character, and it's a shorthand way for companies to avoid having to get to know someone personally before hiring them.

The consequence of this system is that the best jobs go not to those who would perform them best, but to those who are best at playing the game, the people who interview well, the people who dress right, the people who know how to compose a résumé, who know how to keep their head down and toe the line.

Politics is no different. We think we are electing the people who would be the best lawmakers, representatives, leaders, and public servants. Instead, we actually elect the people who have mastered the art of campaigning. Campaigning is not easy, and requires a certain set of skills to succeed at, but these are not the same skills that make a good legislator or president. A successful campaigner must be good at self-promotion, public speaking, geographic targeting, social media, advertising, debate, and ideally should be charismatic, good-looking, and tall (statistics show that the taller candidate usually wins.)

Contrast this with what it takes to be a good legislator. A good legislator must be intelligent, understand the Constitution, have a coherent political philosophy, be able to build coalitions, be good at listening to his constituents and understanding their needs, and be able to resist corruption, bribery, blackmail, and all the various special interests that try to bend gullible lawmakers to their wills. Someone can possess all of the former skills, and yet have none of the latter, which is why so many elections end in disappointment.

We don't elect statesmen; we elect marketing men. And if there's one thing marketing men are good at, it's selling people things they otherwise wouldn't want or need. We can hardly be surprised when such people fail to represent our interests and only look out for themselves.

The problem is compounded by the fact that holding public office involves a great deal of power. There's a reason why independently wealthy tycoons like Donald Trump and Bill de Blasio want to be politicians. It's not for the money, and it's not out of a selfless desire to give something back. It's because politicians can do things that even the richest private citizen could never get away with. Once you've bought your tenth mansion and your eighth yacht, what is there left to do but make the rules by which your fellow citizens will be forced to live? It's the ultimate next step in world domination.

One of the things that remains so impressive about George Washington was his own aversion to political power. He was essentially pressured into becoming the fledgling nation's first President against his will, and when he was offered the chance to become King of America, a position with almost limitless potential and power, he turned it down. Liberty was more important to him than personal gain, and it's why he is remembered so fondly by champions of limited government today.

Unsurprisingly, people with the desire for the kind of power Washington scorned are actually the last ones who should hold it. Running for office, especially if you intend to win, is a grueling, expensive, time-consuming process that takes its toll on a candidate's health and personal relationships. A casual interest in public policy is not going to cut it. You have to be obsessed. You have to want to win that election more that you want anything else in your life. And once you win, it gets even worse.

Incentives of Politicians

If men were angels, no government would be necessary. So wrote James Madison in Federalist 51. The passage is often quoted as evidence that we are just too wicked a species to be trusted or left to our own devices, and that we would be wise to subjugate our freedom to a group of overseers trusted to keep our baser urges in check. Of course, what this analysis leaves out is the obvious fact that the overseers are men themselves, and no more angels than the rest of us. Indeed, as we have already seen, the incentives that drive men into political office hardly encourage the best and brightest to seek the job.

Nevertheless, this idea that the governing class is somehow better, more noble, and more altruistic than the citizenry as a whole is pervasive. It is assumed that those in power are looking out for us, not for themselves. Amazingly, this view was not meaningfully or rigorously challenged until the 20th century, when James Buchanan (the economist, not the president) founded the school known as Public Choice Economics. Buchanan held the surprisingly controversial view that politicians are human beings just like the rest of us, and that they are motivated by the same form of self-interest that drives any common laborer or merchant. The incentives facing elected representatives may be somewhat different, but we should not expect them to respond to those incentives any differently than anyone else would.

So, what are these incentives? The first and most obvious is that, having completed the arduous business of getting into power, politicians want to remain in power. This means always keeping an eye ahead towards the next election. On one hand, this could be seen as a positive thing, as representatives will not want to take actions that anger their constituents, but the realities of campaign financing make this more complicated than it might initially seem. A politician seeking re-election wants to avoid controversial or bold actions, preferring instead to "play it safe" by avoiding tough votes or taking correct, but unpopular stands. He will want to avoid displeasing any major financial interests who could potentially donate to his opponent, and worst of all, he will be tempted to fall in line with his party's leadership. Members who challenge leadership are commonly threatened with the loss of committee assignments, or the deprivation of campaign funds from the party's fundraising apparatus. This encourages the go along to get along attitude that so many find dismaying in Congress.

To give one example, Tim Huelskamp was a firebrand Congressman from Kansas who was always ready to stand on principle and fight for what he believed was right. After he crossed leadership one too many times, however, he was stripped of his position on the House Agriculture Committee. Kansas is a state that relies heavily on federal agriculture policy, and Huelskamp's political opponents were able to convince voters that, without a spot on the Agriculture Committee, Huelskamp wasn't worth electing, and that was the end of his congressional career right there.[41] It's no wonder that so few members are willing to follow their own principles against the

41 "Kansas Regains Seat on House Agricultural Committee," *Associated Press*, January 11, 2017.

Speaker of the House's wishes.

Other incentives faced by politicians include playing ball with special interests to ensure cushy jobs as lobbyists and consultants when their time in office ends, and trading votes for bad policies for the chance to further their own careers. To be clear, I'm not saying that all politicians are bad people, only that they are put into a situation that rewards bad behavior and punishes good behavior. The principled congressman who regards himself as a true public servant generally has nothing to show for his fidelity but a lot of negative press and a bus ticket home, while his colleagues grow rich and powerful off the taxpayer dime.

Our Politicians, Our Masters

America was founded with the noblest of intentions. The Founders wanted to guard against tyranny, and so they abolished the monarchy in favor of a representative government, a democratic republic in which the people would be empowered to govern themselves. But, as anarchist individualist Lysander Spooner once said, "A man is no less a slave because he is allowed to choose a new master once in a term of years."

The terms "representative" and "public servant" are manifest deceptions. The people we elect are not our servants, but our rulers. What else can you call the people who make the laws, have all the most powerful weapons, and can punish us for disobedience in any number of cruel and unjust ways? It is a verbal sleight of hand designed to keep the population docile and under the illusion that they are secretly the ones in charge, while the salaries of their oppressors are extorted from them by force and the threat thereof.

Government, as the monopolist who lays claim to the legitimate use of violence, is the invisible hand behind all the relationships outlined in this book. Neither doctors, nor teachers, nor economists would have very much power over us at all if it were not for the implicit or explicit support of government, the guys with all the guns and prisons.

The next time you hear a politician or bureaucrat assure you that he has your best interest at heart, that he only wants to protect you, that he wants to serve the American people and give something back to his community, ask yourself what kind of servant enjoys such privileges and powers over everyone else in the country. In the last presidential election, the candidates spent a combined total of over $2 billion in campaign funds, and that's not including all the campaigning by outside groups and super-PACS.[42] No one spends that kind of money to serve others. For that amount of money, you expect an awful lot in return.

42 Eli Watkins, "A $2 billion Election, By the Numbers," *CNN*, November 15, 2016.

AFTERWORD: SO WHAT ARE YOU GONNA DO ABOUT IT?

You may feel that the thesis of this book is rather grim. Here, all this time, we thought we were in control of our lives, but it turns out the very people who say they want to help us actually want to control us. How bleak!

I feel your pain. It can be daunting and disillusioning to confront the truth about how manipulative and controlling our fellow humans can be. It can be depressing to realize that we've allowed ourselves to be duped all these years. But do not despair.

Plato used the analogy of a cave to describe the task of philosophy. He regarded the philosopher as one who would lead the people out of darkness and into the light. I do not make any such presumption, nor would I even deign to call myself a philosopher, but what is true is that you can't begin to search for light until you realize that you have been living in darkness. We can't start looking for solutions until we first understand the problem.

What I hope to have accomplished with this book is to point out that things are not as they seem, as a mere starting point on the road towards improving the state of personal liberty, responsibility, and accountability in our society. Maybe some parents will not be so quick to entrust their children to the school system. Maybe some patients will be willing to question medical authority. Maybe some of you will think twice when reading about a new economic study before blindly accepting the conclusion. Maybe some voters will change the way they select and evaluate their local representatives. It is a lot to hope for, but one has to start somewhere.

Information is the first step towards action, and in that vein, let me leave you with one final quotation, one of my all-time favorites from one of the inspirations for this book. Psychiatrist Thomas Szasz, displaying a remarkable command of the language for a non-native speaker, once quipped, "The proverb warns 'do not bite the hand that feeds you', but maybe you should, if it prevents you from feeding yourself."

With that in mind, I would encourage my readers to keep their teeth nice and sharp. They may need them someday soon.

ACKNOWLEDGEMENTS

This book would not have been possible without the generous support of Matt and Terry Kibbe, who were not only kind enough to give me a job, but also to allow me to pursue my wild flights of authorial ambition.

I am, of course, very grateful to all the kind folks at AIER for agreeing to publish this book, preventing it from languishing indefinitely on my hard drive.

Many thanks to my friends and colleagues, including Neil Siefring, who was kind enough to review the manuscript, and Josh Withrow, who not only provided invaluable editorial suggestions, but who also taught me much of what I know about public policy. I also owe much gratitude to Jeffrey Tucker, who has long been a supporter of my writing and was kind enough to offer some advance praise for this book.

Thanks to Trey Grover (or whatever he is calling himself these days) for his encouragement and eagerness to help promote my writing to a broader audience. A special shout-out as well to Mr. Remso Martinez, who graciously invited me to write the foreword to his book, and in so doing inspired me to stop being lazy and write one of my own.

Finally, my eternal and undying gratitude to my parents for their continuing support and steadfast refusal to stop believing in me.

BIBLIOGRAPHY

Part One: Education

Bryan Caplan, *The Case Against Education*

John Taylor Gatto, *Dumbing Us Down*

John Holt, *How Children Learn*

Kirsten Lombard, ed., *Common Ground on Common Core*

Albert Jay Nock, *The Theory of Education in the United States*

Steven Pinker, *The Language Instinct*

Murray Rothbard, *Education: Free and Compulsory*

Herbert Spencer, *Principles of Ethics*

Yong Zhao, *Who's Afraid of the Big Bad Dragon*

Part Two: Economics

Claude Frederic Bastiat, *That Which Is Seen, and That Which Is Not Seen*

Edwin Black, *War Against the Weak*

Walter Block, *Defending the Indefensible*

James Buchanan, *What Should Economists Do?*

F.A. Hayek, *The Counter-Revolution in Science*

F.A. Hayek, *The Fatal Conceit*

Henry Hazlitt, *Economics in One Lesson*

Israel Kirzner, *Austrian Subjectivism*
Carl Menger, *Principles of Economics*
Murray Rothbard, *Classical Economics*
Murray Rothbard, *History of Economic Thought Before Adam Smith*
Murray Rothbard, *Man, Economy, and State*
Adam Smith, *The Wealth of Nations*
Ludwig von Mises, *Epistemological Problems in Economics*
Ludwig von Mises, *Human Action*
Ludwig von Mises, *Socialism*

Part Three: Medicine

Shirley Jackson, *The Lottery*
William James, *Psychology: Briefer Course*
Carl Jung, *The Undiscovered Self*
Irving Kirsch, *The Emperor's New Drugs*
Thomas Szasz, *Insanity*
Thomas Szasz, *The Medicalization of Everyday Life*
Thomas Szasz, *The Myth of Mental Illness*
Thomas Szasz, *Psychiatry: The Science of Lies*

Part Four: Government

Ray Bradbury, *Fahrenheit 451*
James Buchanan, *The Calculus of Consent*
Anthony Burgess, *A Clockwork Orange*
Etienne de La Boetie, *The Politics of Obedience*
Milton Friedman, *Capitalism and Freedom*
F.A. Hayek, *The Road to Serfdom*

John Locke, *The Second Treatise of Government*

John Stuart Mill, *On Liberty*

Robert Nozick, *Anarchy, State, and Utopia*

George Orwell, *1984*

Franz Oppenheimer, *The State*

Steven Pinker, *The Better Angels of Our Nature*

Steven Pinker, *Enlightenment Now*

Ayn Rand, *Anthem*

Ayn Rand, *Atlas Shrugged*

Murray Rothbard, *The Anatomy of the State*

Murray Rothbard, *For a New Liberty*

Herbert Spencer, *The Man versus the State*

Herbert Spencer, *Social Statics*

ABOUT THE AUTHOR

Logan Albright is a Washington, DC-based writer, composer, film-maker and economist currently serving as Director of Research at Free the People Foundation. He received his Master's degree in economics from Georgia State University in 2011, before promptly setting out for DC to join the fight for individual liberty.

Albright first developed these dangerous ideas during his time at Oberlin College, where his contrarian nature drove him into countless hours of heated debate at this bastion of progressive thought. When not railing against the evils of government, Logan enjoys craft beer, weird music, and conspicuous facial hair.

ABOUT AIER

The American Institute for Economic Research in Great Barrington, Massachusetts, was founded in 1933 as the first independent voice for sound economics in the United States. Today it publishes ongoing research, hosts educational programs, publishes books, sponsors interns and scholars, and is home to the world-renowned Bastiat Society and the highly respected Sound Money Project. The American Institute for Economic Research is a 501c3 public charity.

INDEX

Made in the USA
Lexington, KY
11 December 2019

58427557R00126